WRINKLIES™
Classic
Joke Book

First published in Great Britain in 2009
This edition published in 2018 by Prion
an imprint of the Carlton Publishing Group
20 Mortimer Street
London W1T 3JW
2 4 6 8 10 9 7 5 3 1

A catalogue record for this book is available
from the British Library

ISBN 978-1-91161-014-4

Typeset by e-type, Liverpool
Printed in Dubai

WRINKLIES™ Classic Joke Book

Jokes, Gags and One-liners
for the Older Generation

Mike Haskins & Clive Whichelow

PRION

Contents

Introduction	7
You Know You're Getting Old When...	9
Age-old humour	10
The mathematics of ageing	11
Growing old carefully	13
Signs That Your Body Isn't What It Used To Be	17
The spirit is willing...	18
Boys and girls	19
By any other name...	20
Forget-me-not	21
Never too old for a round	23
Quite a mouthful	24
Any old number?	26
Beat the droop	28
Badly bitten	29
Hip, hip, hooray!	32
Positively disappointed	34
You Know You're Getting Old When...	36
Bin there, dun that...	38
Getting catty	39
Ways To Tell If You Are A Wrinklie	41

How To Calculate Your Correct Wrinkly Age –
    Word Association Test   43
Face-ing the future   46
Under the knife   53
Off we go, dear   55
Music to my ears   59
Drive me round the bend!   61
Eatin' out   64
The Perks Of Getting Older And Wrinklier   66
Then and Now   68
So near to thee…   68
Talk is cheap   70
Dazed and confused   73
Green fingers   76
Generation gaps   79
Love and marriage   85
In sickness and in health…   98
You Know You're Getting Old When…   101
Wise old words   103
Not a prayer…   106
Never too late to woo   114
The dating game   115
The cheek of it   123
Sticky situations   125
Things ain't what they used to be   128
Helpful helpers   129
Death and the afterlife   132

No fools   138

Never too old for...   145

Drink and drugs   148

With age comes wisdom, apparently   151

Size isn't everything   153

Money, good looks...   159

Car trouble   161

A dog's life   164

Fair trade...   166

Bits and pieces   170

Oddbods   175

Age and charm...   176

Doctor, doctor   180

Old dogs...   183

Classic Quotes   189

Introduction

Hello wrinklies everywhere!

Although, as you often tell people, they're not really wrinkles, are they? They're laughter lines. Of course this inevitably invites the response, "Surely nothing could be that funny!" But this book could be!

Hopefully reading this will cause eruptions of laughter of an intensity that will make your existing wrinkles pop out – achieving a smooth finish. On the other hand it may cause the formation of enough new wrinkles between your existing wrinkles to create a more consistent overall effect.

The only problem with having that many wrinkles though is that when you laugh, your face will seem to completely disappear into a black hole. But so long as you're happy, who cares!

So keep laughing and keep wrinkling!

Mike Haskins

Note: The authors and publishers will accept no liability for wrinkles induced as a result of reading any joke books or associated works.

You Know You're Getting Old When...

All the cars behind you turn on their headlights.

Your midnight oil is all used up by 9.30pm.

Christmas starts to piss you off.

Complete strangers feel comfortable calling you, "Old-timer".

Conversations with people your own age usually turn into a bout of "ailment duelling".

Even dialling long distance makes you feel tired.

When you're just visiting a friend in hospital, a member of staff comes toward you with a wheelchair.

Every time you suck your belly in, your ankles balloon out.

Everything that works hurts, and what doesn't hurt, doesn't work.

Fortune tellers offer to read your face instead of your palm.

Funeral directors call and make idle conversation about how you're feeling.

Getting a little action means you don't need to eat any fibre today.

Getting lucky means you take less than ten minutes to find your car in the supermarket car park.

Half the stuff in your shopping trolley has the words "for fast relief" printed on the label.

Happy hour is a 30-minute nap.

You start having dry dreams and wet farts.

It gets harder and harder for them to make those sexual harassment charges stick.

It takes longer to rest than it did to get tired in the first place.

It takes you a couple of tries to get over a speed bump.

It takes you longer and longer to get over a good time.

Lawn care has become a highlight of your life.

Age-old humour

She says she's looking forward to her 39th birthday but you can't help thinking she must be looking in the wrong direction.

The mathematics of ageing

Do you realize that the only time in our lives when we like to get old is when we're kids? If you're less than ten years old, you're so excited about ageing that you think in fractions. "How old are you?" "I'm four and a half!" You're never thirty-six and a half. You're four and a half, going on five! That's the key. You get into your teens, now they can't hold you back. You jump to the next number, or even a few ahead. "How old are you?" "I'm gonna be sixteen!" You could be thirteen, but hey, you're gonna be sixteen! And then the greatest day of your life… You become twenty-one. Even the words sound like a ceremony. YOU BECOME twenty-one. YESSSS!!! But then you turn thirty. Oooohh, what happened there? Makes you sound like bad milk! He TURNED; we had to throw him out. There's no fun now, you're just a sour-dumpling. What's wrong? What's changed? You BECOME twenty-one, you TURN thirty, then you're PUSHING forty. Whoa! Put on the brakes, it's all slipping away. Before you know it, you REACH fifty and your dreams are gone. But wait!!! You MAKE it to sixty. You didn't think you would! So you BECOME twenty-one, TURN THIRTY, PUSH FORTY, REACH FIFTY and MAKE it to SIXTY. You've built up so much speed that you

HIT seventy! After that it's a day-by-day thing; you HIT Wednesday! You get into your eighties and every day is a complete cycle; you HIT lunch; you TURN 4:30pm; you REACH bedtime. And it doesn't end there. Into the nineties, you start going backward: "I was JUST ninety-two." Then a strange thing happens. If you make it over one hundred, you become a little kid again. "I'm one hundred and a half!"

George Carlin

∞

When I turned two I was really anxious, because I'd doubled my age in a year. I thought, if this keeps up, by the time I'm six, I'll be ninety.

Steven Wright

∞

When you're three years old, success is not peeing in your pants. When you're eleven, success is having friends. When you're seventeen, success is having a driving licence. When you're twenty, success is having sex. When you're thirty, success is having cash. When you're fifty, success is having money. When you're sixty, success is having sex. When you're seventy, success is having a driving licence. When you're seventy-five, success is having friends. When you're eighty, success is not peeing in your pants.

Growing old carefully

Two old ladies are having a natter about their favourite subject, their various medical conditions. The first tells the second, "The doctor says I need another operation but I can't afford to get it done privately and there's a 12-month waiting list on the NHS." "That's a disgrace," says her friend. "Still never mind. We'll just have to talk about your old operation for another year."

∞

A 90-year-old man goes to his doctor and says, "Oh doctor, I'm having terrible trouble with my right knee. It's awfully stiff and painful." The doctor has a look and says, "I'm afraid there's not much I can do. You have to remember you've had that knee for 90 years now, so you can't expect too much." "What are you talking about?" says the old man. "I've had my left knee for exactly the same length of time and there's nothing wrong with that one at all."

∞

A little old woman lady phones the hospital and says, "Is that the City Hospital? Could you put me through to someone who can give me some information about one of your patients?" "Hold on, please," says the voice at the other end of the line and puts the old lady through. "Hello, can I help you?" says another voice. "Oh yes," says the old lady. "I want to find out how one of your patients is getting on. It's Mrs Elsie Harris and I believe she's in room 302 in the Davenport Ward." "Let me see," says the voice. "Ah yes! Mrs Harris in room 302 in the Davenport Ward. Yes, Mrs Harris is doing very well. She's making a full recovery from her operation, she's had two full meals and her doctor says if she continues improving at this rate, she can go home on Tuesday at 12 o'clock." "That's wonderful news," says the old lady. "Absolutely wonderful!" "From your enthusiasm," says the voice on the phone, "I take it you must be a close relative?" "No," says the old lady, "I *am* Mrs Harris in room 302 on Davenport Ward. I can't get anyone round here to tell me a flipping thing!"

∽

A man walked into a doctor's office and the receptionist asked him what the problem was. He replied, "I've got shingles." She said, "Fill out this form and supply your name and address, medical insurance number. When you're done, please take a seat." Fifteen minutes later a nurse's aide came out and asked him what he had. He said, "I've got shingles." So she took down his height, weight and complete medical history, then said, "Change into this gown and wait in the examining room." Thirty minutes later a nurse came in and asked him what he had. He said, "I've got shingles." So she gave him a blood test, a blood pressure test, an electrocardiogram, and told him to wait for the doctor. An hour later the doctor came in and asked him what he had. He said, "Shingles." The doctor gave him a full-cavity examination, and then said, "I just checked you out thoroughly, and I can't find any sign of shingles anywhere." "No," the man replied. "That's because they're outside in the truck. Where do you want them?"

∞

A posh old woman is talking to her friend. She tells her, "My husband is now so elderly and infirm, I have to watch him all day and night." "But I thought you'd hired a young nurse to take care of him," says her friend. "I have," says the old woman, "that's precisely why I've got to keep an eye on him."

∞

An old man goes to the doctor. "Doctor," he says, pointing to different parts of his body, "when I touch my arm it hurts. When I touch my neck it hurts. And when I touch my stomach it hurts. Do I have some rare disease?" "No," says the doctor, "you have a sore finger."

Grandma was having some stomach problems so the doctor told her to drink tepid water with a teaspoon of Epsom salts an hour before breakfast every morning. After a month she was no better, so went back to the doctor. "Did you drink the water an hour before breakfast every morning?" he asked. "No, doctor," she replied. "I'm sorry but I couldn't manage more than 20 minutes."

In the waiting room at the surgery a vast crowd of people were waiting for their appointments while the doctor seemed to be working at a snail's pace. After two hours' wait, one old man slowly got up and shuffled toward the door. When everyone stopped talking to look at him, he turned and announced, "Well, I think I'll just have to go home and die a natural death."

∞

A 90-year-old man is snoozing in the chair one day when a life insurance salesman knocks at the door. He gives him the hard sell, but the old man is a bit wary about the cost of the insurance which at his age isn't cheap. After about 45 minutes of haggling on the doorstep, the salesman finally says, "Look, I'll tell you what, you have a think about it, sleep on it tonight, and if you wake up in the morning give me a ring, OK?"

∞

When asked in his late nineties if his doctor knew he still smoked, (George) Burns said, "No... he's dead."

Signs That Your Body Isn't What It Used To Be

The doctor asks you to "take off that baggy vest" and you're not even wearing one.

When you run for the bus you're too puffed out to tell the driver what fare you want.

Your waist measurement is bigger than your leg measurement.

The last time you "got on down" at a party you couldn't get up again.

When the doctor asks you to stick your tongue out, you ask him how far is absolutely necessary.

You have more replacements than original bits.

When you get to the gym the first thing you have to do is have a little sit down.

You insist on measuring your waist in inches because centimetres just sounds too depressing.

Combing your hair seems to take less and less time.

You get out of breath coming *down* the stairs.

The spirit is willing...

A woman notices an old man sitting on a park bench sobbing his eyes out. She goes over and asks what's wrong. "I have a 22-year-old wife," says the old man. "Every single morning she insists on making mad passionate love with me before she gets up and makes breakfast for me." "OK," says the woman. The old man goes on, "She makes my lunch for me, does my washing, my ironing, keeps the house beautiful and still has the energy to make love as soon as I get home in the afternoon." "I see," says the woman. "Every evening she cooks me a delicious gourmet meal which she serves with wine and my favourite dessert before doing all the dishes and making love to me again until bedtime." "Fine," says the woman. "So why are you sitting here sobbing?" "I've forgotten where I live," says the old man.

Boys and girls

An elderly couple had dinner at another couple's house, and after eating, the wives left the table and went into the kitchen. The two gentlemen were talking, and one said, "Last night we went out to a new restaurant and it was really great. I would recommend it very highly." The other man said, "What's the restaurant called?" The first man thought and thought then finally said, "What is the name of that flower you give to someone you love? You know... The one that's red and has thorns." "Do you mean a rose?" "Yes, that's the one," replied the man. He then turned toward the kitchen and yelled, "Rose, what's the name of that restaurant we went to last night?"

∞

An elderly couple stop off at a restaurant for lunch. After finishing their meal, they go back to their car and drive away. Unfortunately the elderly lady has forgotten to pick up her glasses from the table and doesn't miss them until they have been driving for half an hour. Her husband fusses and complains constantly as he drives her back. "You're virtually senile," he tells her. "If your memory gets any worse you know what I'll do: I'll put you in a home!" Finally they arrive back, the elderly lady climbs out of the car and walks across to the restaurant. Just as she reaches the door, she hears her husband call out to her, "And another thing: while you're in there, get my hat for me!"

By any other name...

An old actor falls on hard times because he has found it increasingly difficult to remember his lines. After many years he finds a theatre where they are prepared to give him a chance to shine again. The director says, "This is the most important part, and it has only one line. You walk on to the stage at the opening carrying a rose. You hold the rose to your nose with just one finger and thumb, sniff the rose deeply and then say, 'Ah, the sweet aroma of my mistress.'" The actor is thrilled. All day long before the performance, he's

20

practising his line over and over again. Finally, the time comes. The curtain goes up, the actor walks onto the stage, and with great passion delivers the line, "Ah, the sweet aroma of my mistress." The theatre erupts. The audience is screaming with laughter, but the director is steaming! "You fool!" he cries. "You've ruined me!" Bewildered, the old actor asks, "What happened, did I forget my line?" "No!" screams the director. "You forgot the rose!"

Forget-me-not

An elderly gentleman realizes he has been increasingly suffering from hearing problems for a number of years. So he finally decides to go to his doctor to see if he can offer any help. The doctor fits a hearing aid which allows him to hear extremely well once again. One month later the elderly gentleman comes back to see the doctor. The doctor says, "Yes, your hearing is pretty good once again. Your family must be really pleased at the improvement." "Oh I haven't told them about it yet," says the elderly gentleman. "I just sit around and listen to what they're all saying to each other. So far I've changed my will five times!"

∞

An old couple are arguing in bed one night about which of them has become more forgetful. In the end, the old woman tells her husband, "Oh, never mind. Just go and get me a cup of tea, will you? You won't manage to forget that on your way down the stairs, will you?" "Of course not," says the old man. "And don't forget to put in some sugar this time," says his wife. "Will you stop going on at me!" says the old man. "I'm sure I didn't forget to put the sugar in last time." "Yes, you did," says the old woman. "*And* you forgot to put in the milk." "Will you just shut up!" says the old man. "There's nothing wrong with my memory. Now just let me go and get your tea." He plods off down the stairs but a few minutes later he's back again. "I told you," says his wife, very slowly and sternly, "I want a cup of tea with milk and one sugar." "Yes, I know that," says the old man, "but could you just remind me again: how do I get to the kitchen?"

∞

An ageing snake goes to see his doctor. "Doctor, I need something for my eyes," says the snake, "I don't seem to be able to see so well these days." The doctor fixes the snake up with a pair of glasses and tells him to return in two weeks. The snake comes back as requested and tells the doctor he's very depressed. The doctor asks, "What's the problem? Didn't the glasses help you?" "Oh yes," says the snake. "The glasses are fine. But I just found out I've been living with a garden hose for the past couple of years!"

Never too old for a round

Old Jack gets in from a game of golf. "How was it, dear?" asks his wife, Beryl. "Well, I was hitting pretty well, but my eyesight's so bad now I couldn't see where the ball went," he answers. "What can you expect," says Beryl. "You're seventy-five years old!" "I know!" says Jack. "Why don't you take my brother Arthur along?" asks Beryl. "But he's eight-five and he doesn't even play golf," says Jack. "Never mind," says Beryl, "he's got perfect eyesight so he'll be able to watch the ball for you." The next day Jack tees off with Arthur looking on. He takes a swing and the ball disappears down the middle of the fairway. "Did you see where it went?" asks Jack. "I certainly did," replies Arthur. "Excellent," says Jack. "So where is it?" "Er...." says Arthur peering off into the distance. "No, sorry: I've forgotten."

Quite a mouthful

Yes, my teeth are my own! I can show you the receipt if you want.

∞

Two old men go out fishing one day. The sea is quite rough and as a result one manages to lose his dentures over the side of the boat. He was so incensed that his friend decides to play a joke on him. He surreptitiously slips out his own teeth and fixes them onto the end of his fishing line. Then when he hauls the line in with the teeth on the end, he calls out o his friend, "Hey, look what I've caught! It looks like your missing gnashers!" Before he can be stopped his friend unhooks the dentures, tries pushing them into his mouth and then hurls them into the sea with a disgusted cry, "You idiot! Those aren't mine – they don't fit!"

∞

A bus driver is driving along one day when he notices in his mirror that his passengers are all in uproar. He stops the bus and goes to investigate. He discovers an elderly man crawling up and down the bus, looking for something on the floor. "What on earth do you think you're doing?" asks the bus driver. "You're being a nuisance to all the other people on the bus." "I can't help that," says the old man, "I'm looking for my chewing gum." "What do you mean, you're looking for your chewing gum?" says the driver. "You're making this amount of fuss over some old chewing gum that's been on the floor of the bus, which you wouldn't be able to use again anyway." "That doesn't matter," says the old man, "but I've still got to find my chewing gum." "Well, what the hell's so special about this chewing gum?" asks the driver. "My teeth are still in it," says the old man.

∽

An old lady goes to her dentist to have her dentures adjusted for the umpteenth time. Every time she comes back she tells the dentist the same thing, "These dentures still don't fit." "What are you talking about?" says the dentist. "We've adjusted them for you over and over again. How can they possibly still not fit?" "You don't believe they still don't fit, then I'll prove it to you!" says the old woman. "I've brought the tumbler from the side of my bed with me..."

Any old number?

Statistically speaking, by the time you get to the age of seventy there are five women to every one man. It's rather cruel of God to give you that kind of odds at that stage in your life.

∞

When she hears that her elderly grandfather has passed away, a young woman rushes to her grandmother to offer comfort. When she asks how granddad died, her grandmother tells her he had a heart attack while they were making love on Sunday morning. The young woman is shocked and says that two people aged nearly 100 should have realized the dangers of carrying on in such a way. "Oh no!" says granny. "Despite our advanced age we've managed perfectly well for years. We always used to take care by making love in time to the slow chime of the bells in the village church." She paused and wiped away a tear before continuing, "And if it hadn't been for that ice-cream van going past, your granddad would still be alive today."

∞

A young English woman visits America on holiday and goes sightseeing at an Indian reservation. She passes an old Indian and as she walks by, he raises his hand and says, "chance". The woman is puzzled, but walks on. Later she walks back and the old Indian raises his hand again and says, "chance". The woman is intrigued so tries walking past for a third time a bit later. As she does so the old man raises his hand and says "chance" again. She says, "Hello, I hope you don't mind me saying, but I'm from England and I always thought that the Native American greeting was 'how', not 'chance.'" "Lady," says the old Indian, with a twinkle in his eye, "when you get to my age you know how, but the best you can hope for is a chance."

∞

Another of nature's cruel jokes – the menopause (menopause – you just *knew* men would have something to do with it, didn't you?). A lot of men don't even realize their wives are going through the change of life. Yes, they see the mood swings, the odd behaviour, etc, but how are they supposed to know it's not just the usual mood swings and roundabouts? Women of course know all about it, with the hot flushes and everything, but at least it's the end of that dreadful monthly ritual – and no, we're not talking about sex with their husbands!

Beat the droop

What does a 70-year-old woman have between her breasts that a 20-year-old doesn't? Her navel.

∞

I'd love to slit my mother-in-law's corsets and watch her spread to death.

Phyllis Diller

∞

If you're a woman it's not any easier. You get to a certain age, you know you've finished bearing children, all that part of your life is over, perhaps you're not quite so attractive as you once were... and then Mother Nature thinks, "What can I do to improve the quality of this woman's life, how can I help? What can I do for her? What is that magic thing...? I know, a beard!"

Dylan Moran

∞

Have you heard about the new bra they've invented for women in later life? They call it the sheep dog.

That's because it rounds them up and gets them pointing in the same direction.

∞

If you're a woman and you get called in for a mammogram, look on the bright side. At least this is one kind of film they still want you to appear topless in.

∞

Two old ladies are talking one day. One says to the other, "Even though I'm seventy-five men still look at my boobs." "Oh yes," says the second. "I bet they have to squat down a bit first, though."

∞

Old age is when a woman buys a sheer nightie and doesn't know anyone who can see through it!

Badly bitten

The only time a woman wishes she were a year older is when she's expecting a baby.

∞

Two ageing ladies are long-time rivals in their social circle. One year they bump into each other at a Christmas party at their country club. "Why, my dear," says the first, noticing the other's necklace. "Don't tell me those are real pearls?" "Yes, they are," says the second. "You may say that," says the first woman with a thin smile, "but of course the only way I could tell for certain would be to bite them." "Well, I'd be happy for you to do that," says the second woman. "The only trouble is, you'd need real teeth."

∽

A woman is as old as she looks before breakfast.

Edgar Watson Howe

∽

An old man tells his friend, "Despite her age, my wife really doesn't seem to be growing old gracefully. Last week she took part in a wet-shawl contest."

∽

How does an ageing woman manage to keep her youth? By giving him lots and lots of money.

∞

Keith asks his girlfriend Karen to marry him and she says yes, but on one condition: that he buys her a solid gold boy scout knife. He asks around, he looks on the Internet, he tries everywhere, but he can't find a solid gold boy scout knife anywhere. But because he is really keen to marry Karen he goes to a jeweller's and asks them to make one specially. He is told it will be very expensive, but he tells them to go ahead anyway. When it's ready he presents it to Karen, who then agrees to marry him. "So why on earth did you want a solid gold boy scout knife?" asks Keith. "What are you going to do with it?" "I'm going to put it away somewhere safe, then, when I'm old and grey and wrinkled, with half my teeth missing and my boobs sagging, and no man will look at me twice, I'll get it out. Because a boy scout would do almost anything for a solid gold pocket knife."

∞

Q: How is a 50-year-old woman like a used tube of toothpaste?
A: They may be old and wrinkled, but if you squeeze hard enough, you'll find there's something left over.

∞

A middle-aged woman goes to the doctor for a check-up and comes back delighted. "What are you so happy about?" asks her husband. "The doctor said I have the body of a 25-year-old," she replies. "OK," says her husband, "but what did he say about your 45-year-old arse?" "He didn't mention you at all," says the wife sweetly.

Hip, hip, hooray!

You don't know what real embarrassment is like until your hip sets off a metal detector.

∞

An old man goes into hospital to have a hip replacement. The hospital puts in a new plastic one with a sensitive spring-based action. When he gets home his grandchildren are delighted to discover every time they push granddad's head down, he takes a penalty.

∞

Three old men are at the doctor's to have their memories tested. The doctor says to the first old man, "What's three times three?" "Two hundred and seventy-four," was his reply. The doctor worriedly says to the second old man, "It's your turn. What's three times three?" "Tuesday," replies the second old man. The doctor sadly says to the third old man, "OK, it's your turn. What's three times three?" "Nine," says the third old man. "Excellent!" exclaims the doctor. "How did you get that?" "Oh come on, doctor. That was simple," says man. "I just subtracted two hundred and seventy-four from Tuesday."

∞

At the age of seventy Tom starts going to a local senior citizens' exercise club and the instructor says to him one day, "You know, Tom, it's hard to believe you're seventy. From the shape you're in I would have said you were fifty-five at the most. How do you do it?" "Lack of stress," says Tom. "You see, early on in our marriage the wife and I decided that if we ever started to argue then she would go to the bedroom and I'd go out into the garden." "I see," says the instructor, "and how do you think that has helped?" "Well, for the past fifty years" says Tom, "I've been living almost permanently out in the fresh air."

Positively disappointed

A 60-year-old woman is getting some test results at the hospital and the consultant says, "I'm sorry, Mrs Arbuthnot, but you haven't got long to live. I give you 24 hours at the most." Distraught, the woman goes home and says to her husband, "Come on, you, I've only got 24 hours to live. I want you to take me upstairs and make wild passionate love to me all night." He husband looks at her tetchily and says, "It's all right for you, you haven't got to get up in the morning."

∞

A woman accompanied her husband to the doctor's. After his check-up, the doctor called the wife into his office alone. He said, "Your husband is suffering from a very severe disease, combined with horrible stress. If you don't do the following he will surely die. Each morning, make him a healthy breakfast. Try to be pleasant in general, and make sure he stays in a good mood. For lunch, make him a nutritious meal. For dinner, prepare something nice and healthy again. Don't burden him with chores, as he probably had a hard day. Don't discuss your problems with him, it will only make his stress worse. And most importantly, make love with your husband several times a week and satisfy his every whim. If you can do this for the next one to two months, I think your husband will regain his health completely." On the way home, the husband asked his wife, "What did the doctor say?" "You're going to die," she replied.

∞

An old dying man is lying in bed. One day he feels his senses begin to slightly revive as the smell of home baking comes wafting up the stairs and sets his mouth watering. With his last remaining strength, he manages to pull himself out of bed and slowly clambers down the stairs to the kitchen. There he finds his wife has been busy baking a delicious-looking chocolate cake. "Oh, look," says the dying old man, "isn't that lovely? You've gone to the trouble of making me my very favourite cake." Just as he's about to cut himself a slice, his wife suddenly whacks his hand with a wooden spoon. "What's the matter with you?" asks the dying man. "Get your hands off that!" his wife tells him. "That's for the funeral!"

You Know You're Getting Old When...

You find yourself on the stairs and you can't remember if you were downstairs going up, or upstairs going down.

You find yourself taking pleasure in comparative shopping for cemetery plots.

You find yourself telling people what a loaf of bread used to cost.

You get out of the shower and find you're glad the mirror is all fogged up.

You get the same sensation from a rocking chair that you used to get from a roller coaster.

You get tired just watching the fish swim around in the aquarium.

You get two invitations to go out on the same night... and you pick the one that will get you home the earliest.

You get up at night, go to the bathroom and then can't remember why you're there.

You get your full share of exercise acting as a pallbearer for healthy friends who spent all their spare time exercising.

You give up all your bad, unhealthy habits, and you still feel crappy.

You get winded playing chess.

You go into a record shop and wonder why you don't see any records.

You go to a garden party and you're mainly interested in the garden.

You go to a museum and find most of your favourite childhood toys are on display.

You go to a restaurant and complain that the butter is too tough for your teeth.

You go to your local barber's and your local barber asks why.

You have breakfast in bed as a necessity rather than as a luxury.

You have delightful dreams about mouth-watering prunes.

You have more patience, but in reality you just don't care anymore.

You have stopped counting freckles and started tabulating age spots.

Bin there, dun that...

A bin man is on his rounds, collecting the rubbish on his bin lorry. As usual, most of the bins have been left ready on the kerb but one old lady has forgotten to put hers out. Hearing the lorry pass by, she runs out in her dressing gown and curlers, and calls out, "Am I too late for the collection?" "Of course not, love," says the bin man, emptying another load into the back of the truck. "Come on, hop in!"

Junk is something you've kept for years and throw away three weeks before you need it.

As you get older and wrinklier, you spend more and more time trying to look younger. Even if you haven't actually booked a session with Dr Plastic, you'll find that you're now getting more than your money's worth out of the NHS, clocking up zillions of points on your Boots loyalty card and spending a large percentage of your day rubbing in creams, taking potions and vitamins, teasing your last few strands of hair into something approaching a style and generally indulging in some extreme body maintenance. Though when you get to the further extremities of wrinklyhood you may well say, "Oh bugger it, they can take me as I am." You will then be regarded as a charming old eccentric – who whiffs a bit.

Getting catty

A little old lady comes hobbling into an adult goods store looking as though she's suffering some kind of fit. She makes it to the counter and grabs it for support. "D-d--d-d-do y-y-you s-s-s-tock v-v-v-ibrators?" she asks the man on the counter. "Yes," he replies, "we stock vibrators." "D-d-d-do y-y-y-you h-h-h-ave one that's p-p-pink, t-t-tt-twelve inches l-l-l-long and t-t-t-two and a h-h-h-half inches th-th-th-thick?" "Yes," says the man on the counter. "We have that one in stock. Shall I get one for you?"

"N-n-n-n-no," says the old woman, "I d-d-d-don't want to b-b-b-buy one. I w-w-w-want you to t-t-t-tell me h-h-h-how t-t-t-to t-t-t-turn the f-f-f-flipping thing off!"

∞

An old woman comes homes from afternoon bingo one day and finds there's nothing in the fridge for her husband's dinner. It's too late to get any shopping, so she takes a tin of cat food from the cupboard, chops up an onion, adds a few spices and makes the whole lot into a meaty stew. When her husband comes home she gives it to him, and to her amazement he scoffs the lot and says it's delicious. Next day at bingo, she tells her friends what has happened and says she'll try it again as he enjoyed it so much. A couple of weeks later her friends are horrified to find that she is still feeding her husband with cat food. "You'll kill him," they warn her, and sure enough a week later he is dead. Her friends tell her that she should have listened to their warnings. "It wasn't the cat food that killed him," says the woman indignantly, "If you must know, he fell off the fence." "What was he doing up there?" asked one of her friends. "Trying to lick his backside," said the woman.

Ways To Tell If You Are A Wrinklie

OK, you've taken the wrinkly test but you're still not convinced that you're a member of the grey army. You imagine somehow that you've been tricked or conned into outing yourself as a budgie-fancier. In short, you think those tests have been rigged, don't you? You scored highly but you aren't having any of it. You must be in denial. All right, let's get specific. Do you recognize any of the following?

- When you open your bathroom cabinet you realize that the cosmetics are outnumbered by the medicines.

- You find it easier to sit down than to stand up.

- When the binmen ask for a tip at Christmas you say, "Here's a tip – don't drop half the flaming rubbish in the road on your way to the dustcart then you might get a Christmas box!"

- The only downloads you are interested in are regular bowel movements.

- When it's time to go to bed you have the totally irrational wish that the bed could come down to you instead.

- You can't understand why Radio 2 is playing so much rubbishy modern music and has young upstarts like Jonathan Ross presenting shows – disgraceful!

- You fondly reminisce about the days when there were "proper" programmes on the telly and not all this "How Clean Is Your Big Brother Supernany Get Me Out Of Hell's Kitchen Love Island" so-called reality TV (it's all fixed anyway) and if that's reality, I'm glad I'm not long for this world.

- You have one or all of the following on your front door: "No junk mail", "Callers will be asked for ID", "Neighbourhood Watch", "Bugger off", a security chain, a picture of a ferocious-looking dog with the quite transparent porky "I live here" emblazoned underneath.

- You don't need to listen to the weather forecast because you can predict the climate by the noise your joints make as you get out of bed in the mornings.

- You are constantly shocked to find that policeman, politicians and other figures of authority appear to be fresh-faced youths who don't look like they've even started to shave yet.

- You find it impossible to read a newspaper these days without your blood pressure rising to dangerously high levels.

How To Calculate Your Correct Wrinkly Age – Word Association Test

So what's your wrinkly age? Well, you know how old you are because you know when you were born and with a simple bit of mental arithmetic you can work it out. If you're not too old you may even be able to summon up the answer in a flash by memory alone. But age can't just be measured in years; it's about your attitudes to, and perceptions of the world around you. So try this simple quiz and find out.

When the name Brigitte Bardot is mentioned, do you think of:

- a) A sex symbol
- b) An animal rights campaigner
- c) Nothing, because you don't have the foggiest idea who she is

When the word "holiday" is mentioned, do you think of:

a) A lot of faffing around, all for the sake of a change of scenery
b) A nice break from the normal routine
c) Two weeks of sun, booze and sex

When the words "rock music" are mentioned, do you think of:

a) A godawful racket perpetrated by gormless long-haired morons
b) A bit of nostalgia for your long-lost youth
c) The sort of stuff your mum and dad used to listen to before ringtones were invented

When the word "phone" is used, does it conjure up images of:

a) Black bakelite, switchboard operators, the talking clock and red telephone boxes
b) Cold-calling salesman, teenage children chatting for hours and huge bills
c) A mobile entertainment centre, the loss of which would be the equivalent to the loss of a vital organ

When the words "the doctor" are mentioned, do you immediately think:

- a) The man who seemingly holds the balance of your life in his frighteningly young hands
- b) The smug overpaid bloke whose answer to every ailment is a prescription for antibiotics
- c) David Tennant

When the word "pot" is uttered, do you think of:

- a) The emergency convenience under your bed
- b) Your rotund, middle-aged stomach
- c) What your parents used to smoke at university

Asked to name a famous artist, would you be more likely to say:

- a) Rembrandt
- b) Rolf Harris
- c) Banksy

Asked to think of a famous English victory, would you be more likely to say:

- a) World War Two
- b) The 1966 World Cup
- c) It sounds a bit racist, dunnit?

Asked to name a famous duo, would you be more likely to say:

a) Laurel and Hardy
b) Lennon and McCartney
c) Drunk and disorderly

ANSWERS:

Mostly A's – Hmm, you're quite old, aren't you? Either that or you have a few attitude issues to sort out and have been reading too many nostalgia books.

Mostly B's – You're hovering on the precarious verge of wrinkliedom and one large utility bill or yet another reality TV series could push you over the edge – watch out!

Mostly C's – You young whippersnapper! What on earth are you doing reading this book? Shouldn't you be reading some booky wook by Katie Price or something?

Face-ing the future

You know how when some people, as they get older, fail to recognize others – even members of their own family? Well now, due to the wonders of modern cosmetic surgery you can even forget what you used to look like yourself! How fabulous is that? Despite being on the wrong side of middle-age you can wake up in the morning, go into the bathroom and be confronted by a gorgeous, fresh-faced thing with perfect teeth, beautiful hair and a youthful body. Yes, you forgetful old fool, you've forgotten that one of your grandchildren is over to stay!

∽

I don't plan to grow old gracefully. I plan to have face-lifts until my ears meet.

Rita Rudner

∽

A middle-aged man goes to his wife's plastic surgeon to complain. "You've given her a face-lift, a bottom lift, a breast lift and a tummy lift," he says. "So what's the problem?" asks the surgeon. "What's the *problem*?" splutters the man. "She's 18 inches off the flipping ground now!"

∽

A man tells his friend, "Now my wife's getting a bit older, she's getting into all this cosmetic surgery and beauty treatment business. Yesterday she was at the beauty clinic for over two hours. And that was just for the estimate."

∞

An ageing woman is worrying about the cosmetic surgery she has booked. "Is it going to hurt?" she asks her doctor. "Yes," he says, "but not until you receive my bill."

∞

A definition of unhappiness: a woman who has her face lifted only to find an identical one lurking underneath.

∞

A 60-year-old man decides to have a face-lift for his birthday. He spends £10,000 and is really happy with the results. On his way home, he stops at a newsagent and buys a paper. While he's there, he asks the sales assistant, "I hope you don't mind me asking, but how old do you think I am?" "About forty," says the sales assistant. "I'm actually sixty," says the man feeling very pleased with himself. After that, he goes into a chip shop for some lunch and asks the assistant there the same question. The assistant says, "I'd say about thirty-five." "Thanks very much," says the man, "I'm actually sixty." Later, while he's waiting at a bus stop, he asks an old woman the same question. She replies, "I'm eighty-five years old, and my eyesight is going. But when I was young, there was a sure way of telling a man's age. If I have a feel in your pants for a minute, I will be able to tell you your exact age." As there was no one around, the man lets her slip her hand down his pants. Ten minutes later, the old lady says, "Right, you're sixty years old." "That's incredible," says the man, "you're exactly right. How do you do that?" "I was behind you in the chip shop," says the old lady.

∞

Advice for wrinklies trying to get rid of the wrinkles: I don't know much about plastic surgery but a good rule of thumb is that you know it's time to stop when you look constantly frightened.

∞

The best way to prevent sagging: just eat till the wrinkles fill out.

∞

Two men are sitting in a pub and opposite them is an attractive, young-looking woman sitting on her own, sipping a glass of wine. One of the men indicates the woman and says, "I reckon that woman has had a face-lift, you know." The other one says, "How can you tell?" And the first man replies, "Every time she crosses her legs, her mouth suddenly closes."

∞

A famous old actor was bemoaning his lot on a chat show: "Some women get their good looks from their mothers. Mine gets hers from the plastic surgeon – and it's costing me a fortune!"

∞

A woman with terrible bags under her eyes finally decides to do something about it so she goes to a plastic surgeon and asks him to get rid of them.

He performs the operation and tells the woman afterwards that to save her from having to keep coming back in years to come he has fixed a discreet handle to the back of her neck. "If those bags start coming back," he says, "just turn the handle a bit and it'll tighten up your skin and the bags will just disappear like magic." "Well, thank you," says the woman, delighted. Every so often, when the bags under her eyes begin to show, she turns the handle and they disappear, but after many years two bags appear which are just impossible to remove, however much she turns the handle, so she goes back to the surgeon. He takes a look and says, "Madam, those aren't eye bags – they're your breasts. You've been turning that handle too hard." "Oh my goodness!" exclaims the woman. "I suppose that'll explain the goatee as well."

∾

A man tells his friend, "My wife went in for a face-lift operation last week." "Did it work?" asks the friend. "Not really," says the man. "When they saw what was under it, they dropped it again."

∾

51

Two women are sitting in the old people's home bitching about the other inmates. One old lady says to the other, "Look at her, she's had her face lifted so often, when she raises her eyebrows her bedsocks shoot up her legs."

Edna is a 45-year-old woman. One day she has a heart attack and is taken to hospital. While on the operating table she has a near-death experience. Seeing God she asks, "Is this it? Is my time up?" God replies, "No, Edna, my child. You have come here too soon. In fact, you have another forty-three years, two months and eight days to live." Upon recovery, Edna decides to stay in the hospital and have a face-lift, liposuction, breast implants and a tummy tuck. She even has someone come in and change her hair colour and brighten her teeth! Well, she thinks to herself, since I have so much more time to live, I may as well make the most of it. After all her cosmetic surgery and treatment, she gets out of hospital but, while crossing the street on her way home, she is run over by an ambulance and killed. She arrives up in Heaven in front of God and is completely furious. "What's going on?" she asks God. "I thought you said I had another forty-three years? Why didn't you pull me from out of the path of the ambulance?" "Oh, sorry, Edna," replies God, "I didn't recognize you!"

Under the knife

These days there's not so much stigma attached to having cosmetic surgery though there's a hell of a lot attached to looking old. In fact it's virtually illegal in some quarters. How many supermodels can you name over forty? How many can you name over thirty come to that? And no, we're not talking about their IQ. How many Hollywood actresses get to the age of fifty without a spot of nip and tuck? And have you ever seen a pole dancer dancing round her walking stick – even if half the audience have brought theirs? Exactly. So more and more people are resorting to the surgeon's knife to enhance their sagging features. But it's not cheap, so here are a few handy hints on how to look heavenly without spending the earth.

The beginnings of a fat tummy? Join a weight-watchers club and do nothing. Simply by walking through the door and mixing with the lumps of lard on display you will immediately look and feel thinner.

Bags under the eyes? You may remember a punk singer by the name of Siouxsie Sioux, or if you were too old even then, how about Dusty Springfield? Each of them seemed to finish off a tub of mascara and eye shadow every morning. They had so much make-up round their eyes that they managed to make pandas look understated. But the point is that no one knew whether they had bags under their eyes beneath that lot. In fact you weren't even sure whether they had eyes beneath that lot. So, keep 'em guessing with the black stuff!

∽

Lines on face? Everyone these days has tattoos. They're not just for the likes of sailors and builders anymore. Many people have them on their faces too, so get your friendly neighbourhood tattooist to expertly link the lines with tattoo ink and create a fabulous design – how about one of those low-depression weather maps with a couple of little clouds and a sun thrown in, or an aerial view of the windswept sands of the Sahara?

You might even set a new trend!

∽

Unsightly nose? Become a clown. Does anyone laugh at a clown because he has a bulbous red nose? Does anyone laugh at a clown full stop? But whatever the shape of the offending proboscis it will be skilfully masked by the addition of Coco's conk. All together now, "I wish it could be Red Nose Day every day-i-yay!"

∞

Flabby bottom? Even if you could afford liposuction, would you really want to witness your excess fat being sucked up the end of a glorified hoover? No, neither would we, thank you very much. The trick is to become a mechanic. No mechanic alive has ever found a set of overalls that will fit, so having a couple of spare yards of grease-stained denim flapping round your backside will not look odd in the slightest. And you won't have to pay to have your car serviced any more. Double bubble!

Off we go, dear

An old man is trying to get his reluctant old friend to come out for a walk. "What happened to your get-up-and-go," he asks. "It got up and went without me," says his friend.

An old couple arrive at the airport just in the nick of time to catch the plane for their summer holiday. "Do you know what?" says the old lady. "I wish I'd brought the piano with us." "What on earth are you talking about?" says her husband. "Why would you want to bring the piano with you." "Because," says the old lady, "I've left our tickets on top of it."

⚮

Albert and Henry are taking a stroll along the sea front one day when a seagull flies over and drops a blob of excrement right on the top of Albert's bald head. Henry is horrified at what has just happened and says in great concern, "Wait right there. I'll be back in a moment." He waddles off as fast as he can go to the nearest public convenience and returns a few minutes later with a length of toilet paper. "It's a bit too late for that," says Albert. "That seagull will be miles away by now."

⚮

Cliff and his wife Esther go to their local county fair every year and every year Cliff tells his wife, "You know what I'd really like to do? I'd like to ride in that helicopter they've got over there." And every year Esther replies, "Cliff, you know very well that they charge £50 a ride. That's a lot of money to us pensioners." Finally Cliff tells Esther, "Esther, look, I'm eighty-five years old. If I don't get a ride in that helicopter this year, I might never get another chance." "Cliff," says his wife, "I've told you, £50 is a lot of money to pensioners like us." The helicopter pilot happens to hear the old couple's conversation and says to them, "OK, I'll make you a deal with you. I'll take the both of you for a ride. If you can stay quiet for the entire trip and not say a word, I won't charge you! But if you say one word, I'll have to charge you £50." Cliff and Esther agree and up they go in the helicopter. The pilot does all kinds of fancy manoeuvres, but doesn't hear a word from the couple. He does some daredevil tricks over and over again, but still not a word from the back. When they land, the pilot turns to Cliff and says, "Goodness me, I did everything I could to get you to scream back there, but you didn't. I'm impressed!" Cliff replies, "Well, to tell you the truth, I almost said something when Esther fell out, but you know... £50 is a lot of money to pensioners like us."

At the seaside there are two old men on their annual holidays standing in the sea with their trousers rolled up, smoking their pipes and watching the boats go by. One of them glances down at the other one's feet and says, "Blimey, mate, look at the state of your feet, they're absolutely filthy!" The other looks down and agrees, "Yeah, I know," he says. "We didn't manage to get here last year."

∞

Two old men are looking round a National Trust property when one says to the other, "You know, visiting these historical sites isn't so much fun when they all turn out to be younger than you are."

∞

One night, at the lodge of a hunting club, two new members were being introduced and shown around. The man guiding them said, "See that old man asleep in the chair by the fireplace, he's our oldest member and can tell you some hunting stories that you'll never forget." They woke the old man up and asked him to tell them a hunting story. "Well, I remember back in 1944," said the old man, "we went on a deer hunt in Canada. We were on foot

and hunted for three days without seeing a thing.
On the fourth day, I was so tired I had to rest my
feet. I found a tree that had fallen, so I laid my gun
down, propped my head on the tree, and fell asleep.
I don't remember how long I slept, but I remember
the noise in the bushes that caused me to wake up.
I was reaching for my gun when the biggest buck
that I had ever seen jumped out of the bushes at me
like this WHOOOOHHHHHH!!!!!!!!!!!!........ I tell
you, I just filled my pants." The young men looked
astonished and one of them said, "I don't blame
you! I would have filled my pants too if a huge buck
jumped out at me." The old man shook his head
and said, "No, no, not then, just now when I said
WHOOOOHHHHHH!!!!!!!!!!!"

Music to my ears

Two old ladies were sitting in the park enjoying some
music. "I think it's a minuet from Mignon," said one.
"I thought it was a waltz from Faust," said the other.
So the first old lady got up and shuffled over to a
nearby noticeboard. "We were both wrong," she said.
"It's a Refrain from Spitting."

A plane has a rough flight over the ocean. Suddenly a voice comes over the intercom: "Ladies and gentlemen, please fasten your seat belts and assume crash positions. We have lost our engines and we are trying to put this baby down as gently as possible on the water." "Oh stewardess! Are there any sharks in the ocean below?" asks a little old lady, terrified. "Yes, I'm afraid there are some. But not to worry, we have a special gel in the bottle next to your chair designed especially for emergencies like this. Just rub the gel onto your arms and legs." "And if I do this, the sharks won't eat me any more?" asks the lady. "Oh, they'll eat you all right, only they won't enjoy it so much," answers the stewardess.

∞

Two old golfing partners are at the airport, booking a flight. One of them says, "Do you think we should take out any insurance?" "No," replies the other one. "I never bother any more. I used to, but it never seemed to make the slightest bit of difference."

Drive me round the bend!

A senior citizen was out driving his brand new BMW convertible down the motorway. He put his foot down and went up to 90 miles per hour, enjoying the wind blowing through what little hair he had left. "Amazing!" he thought as he flew down the motorway, but then he noticed in his rear-view mirror, the flashing blue light of a police car as it sped up to catch him. "I can get away from him – no problem!" thought the old man, speeding up to a 110mph, then 120mph and then 130mph. Suddenly, he thought, "What on earth am I doing? I'm too old for this nonsense!" So he pulled over to the side of the road and waited for the police car to catch up with him. Pulling in behind him, the police officer walked up to his window, looked at his watch and said, "Sir, my shift ends in 15 minutes. Today is Friday and I'm taking off for the weekend. If you can give me a reason why you were speeding that I've never heard before, I'll let you go." The man looked very seriously at the policeman, and replied, "Years ago, my wife ran off with a policeman. I thought you were bringing her back." There was a short pause before the policeman said, "Have a good day, sir."

A young man in a Ferrari stops at a red light and notices an ancient old man on an even more ancient old moped pull up next to him. The old man looks over at the Ferrari and says, "Nice car. Mind if I take a look inside?" "No problem," replies the owner. So the old man pokes his head in the window and looks around. Then, sitting back on his moped, the old man says, "That's a pretty nice car, all right!" Just then the light changes so the guy decides to show the old man just what his car can do. He floors it, and within a few seconds his speedometer has reached over 150mph. Suddenly, he notices a dot in his rear-view mirror. It seems to be getting closer! He slows down to see what it could be and suddenly, whoosh! Something whips by him, going much faster than he is! "What on earth could be going faster than my Ferrari?" the young man asks himself. Then, ahead of him, he sees a dot coming toward him. Whoosh! It goes by again, heading in the opposite direction! And it looked like the old man on the moped! "It can't be!" thinks the young guy. But when he looks in his rear-view mirror he sees it approaching again at incredible speed and with another whoosh it ploughs straight into the back of his car. The young man jumps out and sees that it *is* the old man on a now badly mangled moped. He runs round to the old fellow and says, "Is there anything I can do for you?" "Yes, please," whispers the old man. "Could you unhook... my braces ...from your side-view mirror..."

∞

There is a long tailback on the motorway and a police car passing on the other side notices it's caused by a car doing 20 miles an hour. The two policemen eventually stop the offending vehicle and inside they discover two little old ladies, one driving and one sitting in the passenger seat, looking shaken and white as a sheet. "Now, madam," says one of the policemen to the driver, "why were you going so slowly?" "I always go at the speed that it says on the sign," explained the old woman. "And what sign was that, madam?" asks the second policeman. "It said M20," explained the little old lady. "So I did 20 miles an hour the same way I did 31 miles an hour on the A31, then 40 miles an hour on the A40, and..." "And what's wrong with your friend?" the policeman asks, referring to the passenger who is still staring blankly into space, clutching onto the seat for dear life. "Oh, you won't get any sense out of her," says the driver, "she's been like that ever since we came off the A159."

Eatin' out

A little old couple slowly hobble into a fast food
restaurant one cold winter's evening. The old lady
takes a seat, while the little old man goes to the
counter and orders a meal. The old man takes his
food back to the table, sits down, unwraps his burger,
cuts it in half and places one half in front of his wife.
He then carefully divides the French fries into two
piles and places one in front of his wife. The old
man then takes a sip of the drink and begins to eat.
The old couple and their meagre meal attract pitying
looks from other diners and a young man goes to
ask them if they would like another burger and fries,
so they don't have to share. "No thanks, sonny,"
says the old man. "We're used to sharing. We share
everything." The young man then notices that the
little old lady still hasn't touched her food and is just
sitting there watching her husband eat occasionally
and sip some of the drink. Again the young man
asks if he can buy them another meal. "No thank
you, young man," says the old lady. "We're used to
sharing. We share everything." "But you're not eating
anything," says the young man. "Don't you like it?
Shall I get you something else?" "No," replies the
old lady. "This will be fine. In fact I can't wait to get
stuck in." "Then what are you waiting for?" asks

the young man. "I'm waiting," says the old woman with a big toothless smile, "for him to finish with the dentures."

∞

An old man goes into a restaurant one day. He looks at the menu and orders, "just a bowl of soup and some bread." The old fellow eats his soup and bread but when the restaurant manager asks him if he enjoyed his meal, he says, "Yes. It was quite passable but you're a bit mean with the bread aren't you? I only got two pieces." The next day, the old man turns up at the restaurant again and orders exactly the same meal. This time the manager gives him four pieces of bread but still when he asks him if he enjoyed the meal, the old man replies, "Yes. It was quite passable but I just can't understand why you're so mean with the bread." When the old fellow returns again the next day, the manager is determined to give him enough bread. This time he gives him eight pieces with his soup but still the old man tells him, "It was quite passable but I still could have done with more bread." The restaurant manager is now completely exasperated by the fussy old man's behaviour but he refuses to be beaten. So when the old man returns the next day and orders his soup and bread, the manager produces a huge, six-foot French loaf that he's had the bakery next door prepare specially. The manager serves the old man his soup, produces a chainsaw to slice the gargantuan French loaf and heaves the bread up onto the man's table. Incredibly the old man manages to eat not only his soup but the huge loaf of bread as well. As he goes to pay, the manager asks him, "So? How was your meal today?" "It was passable. Quite passable," says the old man. "But I just can't believe you're so mean with the bread." "What the hell are you talking about?" squeals the manager in despair. "Well," says the old man, "I notice you've gone back to serving only two pieces now."

The Perks Of Getting Older And Wrinklier

All that money you've been investing in the NHS over the years will now finally start to pay off.

If you've never smoked, what the hell? Why not start? What's the worst that can happen?

In a hostage situation they're more likely to keep the young, pretty ones.

In general, kidnappers will be less interested in you.

Nobody will expect you to run a marathon.

Nobody will expect you to run into a burning building.

You can buy things now and know they will never wear out.

You can eat your dinner at four in the afternoon and not feel ridiculous.

You can enjoy heated arguments about pension plans with your friends.

You can stop trying to hold your stomach in, even if a supermodel walks into the room.

You get to hear all about other peoples' operations.

You no longer have to think of a speed limit as a challenge.

Your doctor will no longer immediately dismiss you as a hypochondriac.

Your eyes won't get much worse.

You've finally got your number of brain cells down to a manageable size.

You've got nothing left to learn the hard way.

Then and Now

Then: Dreaming about one day having a BMW. Now: Dreaming about one day having a BM.

Then: Killer weed. Now: Weed killer.

Then: Taking acid. Now: Taking antacid.

Then: The perfect high. Now: The perfect high-yield mutual fund.

So near to thee...

As people come to the end of their life they often feel compelled to finally tell the truth and go to meet their maker with a clear conscience. Which is all very well unless the truth happens to be, "Thanks for nursing me all these years through my terrible illness, but I have to tell you we're not actually related. I came to read the gas meter in 1964, had a cup of tea with your mum, one thing led to another, and I never got round to leaving, so I'm leaving all my money to the boilermaker's union and..."

An old man is lying on his deathbed with his wife sitting near him. He says, "Dear wife, I must confess certain things to you before I die." She says, "Hush now, husband, you're fading fast." He says, "But this is really important, I must tell you so I can die with a clear conscience! I slept with your best friend, your sister, and your mother!" She says, "I know. Of course I know all about it." "You do?" says the old man. "Of course," says his wife. "Why do you think I poisoned you?"

❧

Another old man is on his deathbed and his wife too is talking to him in his last hours. "Tell me," says the husband, "I've never asked this before because it's so awkward, but I can't go to my grave without knowing." "What is it?" asks his concerned wife. "Three of our sons are tall with straight red hair," says the husband, "but little Adam is short with curly blond hair. Tell me, is he really my child?" "Of course he is, darling," says the wife, and the husband closes his eyes, turns over and dies peacefully. "Thank goodness he didn't ask about the other three," says the wife.

Talk is cheap

Four elderly ladies are sitting playing bridge. The first lady says, "Girls, I've known you all many years and there's something I've got to get off my chest. I'm a kleptomaniac. But don't worry, I've never stolen from any of you and I never will." The second lady pipes up, "Well, since we're confessing all, I must tell you I'm a nymphomaniac. But don't worry, I've never tried to seduce your husbands and I never will." "Well," says the third lady. "I've something to confess too. I'm a lesbian. But don't worry, you're not my type." The fourth lady stands up. "I must confess," she says, "I'm an incurable gossip, and I've just got some phone calls to make."

∞

An elderly Italian man goes to confession. "Father," he says to the priest, "I need to unburden my guilty conscience." "Very well," says the priest, "what's the problem?" "Well," says the old man, "during the war, a beautiful Jewish woman knocked on my door and asked me to hide her from the Germans. I hid her in my attic, and they never found her." "Why would you feel guilty about such a thing?" says the priest. "That was a wonderful thing you did." "But, father," says the old man, "I was weak and I told her that she must repay me for this kindness by performing sexual favours, which she did." "I see," says the priest. "You shouldn't have taken advantage of the poor woman. But nevertheless you did a good deed in saving her life. Say five Hail Marys." "Thank you, father. That's a tremendous weight off my mind," says the old man. "But there's just one other thing…" "What's that?" asks the priest. "Do I need to tell her the war is over?" asks the old man.

∞

An old man walks into a church to make his confession. "Forgive me father, for I have sinned," says the old man. "I am 80 years old and I was walking home from the pensioners' dinner club the other day when a couple of 20-year-old girls stopped their car and said they needed directions. We got into a discussion and they offered to drive me home and on the way, one of them asked me the last time I'd had sex and I told them it had been years, and she said, would I like to have some fun and before I knew it, we were all in my bed performing the most erotic shocking acts I've ever known." The priest sits tutting through all this. Finally he asks, "OK, so how long is it since your last confession?" "Never," says the old man. "I'm Jewish." "What do you mean?" says the priest. "If you're Jewish, why are you telling me all this?" "I'm not just telling you," says the old man, "I'm telling *everyone*."

∞

A new young priest is nervous about hearing confessions so he asks his older more experienced colleague to sit in on his sessions. The new priest hears a few confessions but then the old priest asks him to step out of the confessional for a moment. "OK," says the old priest, "when you hear confessions, try crossing your arms over your chest and rubbing your chin with one hand. It'll make it look like you're deep in thought." The new priest tries this. Then the old priest suggests, "Also, try saying things like, 'I see, yes, go on,' and 'I understand', or 'How did you feel about that?'" The new priest takes these suggestions on board as well. "And finally," says the old priest, "when you're hearing people confess their private, most intimate sins, try not to keep slapping your knee and saying, 'Wow! Cool, man! So what happened next?'"

Dazed and confused

An eminent and rather pompous QC is out shooting in the country. He brings down his first pheasant and it lands in the next field. He spots an old farmer nearby and calls out, "Hey you! Pass me that bird, would you?" The old farmer says, "No. This be moi field, so this be moi bird." "Now come on!" says the QC. "Be a good chap and pass it over, will you?" "Round these here parts," says the farmer, "we settles our disputes with the 'three whacks' rule." "What's that?" asks the QC. "Well, oi whacks you three toimes with moi stick," says the farmer, "and you whacks me three toimes with your stick, and whomsoever whacks the hardest is declared the winner." "Oh, all right then," says the QC, and the farmer climbs over the stile and gives the QC three almighty whacks with his stick, knocking him to the ground. The QC stands up, dusts himself off and says breathlessly, as he brandishes his stick, "OK, chum. Now it's my turn." "No, you're all roight," says the farmer, "you can keep the rotten bird."

∞

A young man is walking round a supermarket one day when he notices an old lady following him around. He ignores her at first but when he gets to the checkout, he finds her in the queue in front of him. "Pardon me," she says. "I'm sorry if I've been staring, but you look so much like my son who died recently." "I'm sorry to hear that," says the young man. "Is there anything I can do for you?" "Well," says the old lady, "this may sound silly to you but if you could just call me mother, it would make me feel so happy. Just say, 'Goodbye, mother!' as I'm walking out of the shop." "Of course," says the young man, "it's the very least I can do." And so just as the old lady is collecting her shopping bags from the end of the checkout, he says, "Goodbye, mother!" before she walks out of the shop. When he comes to pay, he finds his bill is £100 more than he expected. "It can't be that much," he says. "I only bought a couple of things." "I know that," says the cashier, "but your mother said you would pay for her shopping as well."

∞

An old man meets up with one of his friends from his younger days who had always suffered from a terrible stammer. The old man is astonished to see his stuttering friend now dressed in an expensive suit and driving a Rolls-Royce. "You seem to have done well in life," says the old man. "What line of business did you end up in?" "I s-s-s-sold Bibles d-d-d-door to d-d-d-door," says his friend. "You managed to make good money selling Bibles door to door?" says the old man. "How on earth did you do that?" "W-w-well," says his friend. "I j-j-just kn-kn-kn-knocked on p-p-p-p-p-p-p-peoples' d-d-d-d-doors, and said, 'H-h-h-hello. Do you w-w-want to b-b-b-buy a B-B-B-Bible? If you don't w-w-want to b-b-b-buy a B-B-B-Bible, I can always j-j-j-just r-r-r-read it to you!"

❧

Jason is walking across the common one day when he sees a little old man sitting on a bench nowhere near any water, dangling a fishing rod over the grass. Intrigued, he goes up to the old man and asks him what he's doing. "Fishing," says the old man. Deciding to humour him, Jason asks, "And what were you hoping to catch today?" "Just something for my lunch," says the old man. Jason feels sorry for the poor deluded old codger and says, "Come on! Come with me and I'll buy you a nice lunch." So he takes him to a restaurant and they enjoy a large mixed grill, a beautiful pudding, a bottle of wine and coffees. As he pays the bill and leaves the restaurant, Jason says to the old man, "That was better than anything you'd find out there on the common, wasn't it? I mean, do you ever catch much out there?" "To be honest," says the old man, "you're the third one today."

∞

The hardest years in life are those between ten and seventy.

Helen Hayes

Green fingers

When you're young you play in the garden, when you're a bit older you lie in the garden, and when you're properly grown up and middle-aged you suddenly find you can grow stuff out there too! Also, it gives you the fabulous opportunity of having something new to moan about. "If that cat from next door poops on my tomato plants again I'll get my air rifle out of the loft!", "Ooh, I think I've pulled something planting those hollyhocks," "If it wasn't for this bloomin' climate change I'd have won the prize pumpkin category hands down." And so on. See? You wouldn't have half the fun of middle-age if it wasn't for a spot of gardening.

A vicar is walking through his parish one day and stops to admire an area that an elderly parishioner has turned from a piece of wasteland into a beautiful garden. "Ah," says the vicar, "It's so inspiring what man can achieve with the help of the Almighty." "Yes," replies the old man. "But you should have seen the mess it was in when He had it all to Himself."

Did you hear about the keen gardener who managed to give himself a double hernia last week lifting his huge prize marrows? He's turned his attentions to pumpkins and has developed two new strains.

Two old men are down at the allotments comparing notes when one says, "What do you put on your rhubarb then, Arthur?" "Fresh horse manure," replies Arthur, "you can't beat it." "Oh yes," replies his friend, "to be honest with you, I prefer custard."

Two elderly women gardeners enter their carrots in the village vegetable show. One is declared the winner and starts crowing about her success. "Well, I'm not surprised I won, to be honest," she says. "Your carrots were a bit on the small side quite frankly." "That's true," says the other woman. "Mind you, I did grow them to fit my mouth, not yours."

∞

An old Muslim man living in London plants some potatoes in his back garden. However, when the time comes to dig them up, he finds the work is too hard for him. He emails his son in Pakistan and asks for his advice. "Don't worry, Dad," replies the son. "I'll take care of it." Two hours later there's a squeal of brakes outside the old man's house and a squad of armed police officers run in and start digging up the potato patch. When they've dug it all up, they give the old man a look and drive off. The old man is intrigued until he notices a new message in his inbox saying, "I've buried the stuff in the potato patch. You know what to do."

∞

Did you hear about the elderly man who got stuck out in his allotment during the recent snowy weather? When they eventually dug him out they found him frozen to the marrow.

∞

A man and his wife are looking out of the back window at their vegetable patch in the back garden. The wife turns to the husband and says, "You know, Bert, sooner or later you're going to have to make a proper scarecrow for this place." "Why?" asks her husband. "Because," she says, "your mother's arms must be getting awfully tired by now."

Generation gaps

Why do grandchildren get on so well with their grandparents? They both have a common enemy.

∞

Grandchildren are God's reward for not killing your children.

∞

It's not the arrival of grandchildren that suddenly makes a man feel old. It's the sudden realization that he's married to a grandmother.

∞

A little boy goes to his best friend's house in the morning so they can walk along to school together. When his friend comes out he sees him saying goodbye to an old lady. "Who was that old lady in your house?" asks the little boy. "That's my grandmother," says his friend. "She's come to stay with us for a few weeks." "Where does she usually live?" asks the little boy. "At the big train station in the city," says his friend. The little boy is astonished. "She lives in the big train station in the city!" he says. "Yes," says his friend. "Whenever we want her, we just go along there and get her."

∞

Little Billy is very happy to see his grandmother come to visit again. He runs up, gives her a hug and tells her, "I'm so happy to see you, Grandma. Now Daddy will have to do that trick he's been promising to do." "What trick is that, dear?" asks his grandmother. "Well," says little Billy, "Daddy told us

80

he would climb up the flipping wall if you came to visit us again."

❧

An elderly man shuffles into a toy shop and points out an expensive model train set in the window. "Oh yes," says the shop assistant, "I'm sure your grandson will love playing with this, sir." "Oh yes, that's a point," says the old man. "You'd better give me two."

❧

One Christmas a mother decides that she can't be bothered badgering her children to write thank-you notes for their presents. The result is that their old granddad doesn't receive any thank-you notes for any of the generous cheques he has sent. The next year things are slightly different and granddad receives a visit from all of his grandchildren, who come to thank him in person for their cheques. "That's nice to see, isn't it?" says their mother. "At last it seems they've learnt their manners." "It could be that," says granddad. "On the other hand, it could be the fact that this year I didn't sign the cheques before I sent them."

Every Saturday morning granddad had to baby-sit his three little grandsons. The boys always wanted to play "war", and granddad always got coaxed into playing along. His daughter came to pick up the children one Saturday and saw granddad get shot by one of the boys using a toy gun. Granddad slumped to the floor and lay there motionless. The daughter rushed over to see if he was all right. Granddad opened one eye and whispered, "Shh, I always do this. It's the only chance I get to have a bit of a rest."

∞

A grandmother buys a toy water cannon for her three-year-old grandson. When the little boy opens his present his dad says to the grandmother, "I'm really surprised you'd buy him something like that. Don't you remember how I used to drive you mad, firing my water cannon at you when I was little?" "Yes," says the grandmother with a wicked smile. "I remember very well indeed."

∞

A little boy runs up to his granddad and asks him, "Granddad, do you think you could do a frog impression for Mummy and Daddy?" "Why do they want me to do that?" asks Granddad. "I don't know," says the little boy, "but they were just saying we're all going to go on holiday to Disneyland as soon as you croak."

❧

A grandmother was helping to teach her young granddaughter the names of different colours. So everywhere they went she would point something out, ask the little girl what colour it was and the little girl would answer. After a little while of doing this the little girl was beginning to get them right each time but still the grandmother carried on asking her the colours of different things until the little girl finally turned to her and said, "Grandma, I really think you should try and work some of these out for yourself!"

❧

A little boy goes to his daddy and asks, "Daddy, why does Grandma read the Bible all the time?" "Because, son," says Dad, "your grandmother's currently cramming for her finals."

❧

A teenage granddaughter comes downstairs for her date wearing a see-through blouse and no bra. Her grandmother has a fit when she sees this and tells her not to go out like that. The teenager tells her, "Don't tell me what to do. Things have changed since your day. You've got to let your rosebuds show!" The next day the teenager comes downstairs and the grandmother is sitting there with no top on.
The teenager wants to die with embarrassment.
She explains to her grandmother that she has friends coming over and dressing like that is simply inappropriate. The grandmother says, "Look, dearie. If you can show off your rosebuds, then surely I can display my hanging baskets."

∞

Little Samantha's grandmother comes round for tea one day. All through the meal Samantha stares at her without saying a word. "Samantha!" says her mother, rather embarrassed. "It's very rude to stare. Aren't you going to say anything to your granny?" "Granny," Samantha finally says, "how come your skin doesn't fit your face?"

∞

A little boy is staying with his grandparents for a few days. While he's there he makes friends with the family next door, who have children his age. After an afternoon playing with them he comes back and asks his grandmother, "Grandma, what do you call that thing when two people sleep together and one of them goes on top of the other?" "Oh my goodness," says the grandmother. She is rather taken aback, but decides to tell him the truth. "It's called sexual intercourse, dear." The little boy says, "OK" and runs back to the house next door. A few minutes later he comes back again and tells her, "Grandma, you were wrong. It is not called sexual intercourse. It's called bunk beds. Oh, and Timmy's mum would like a word with you!"

Love and marriage

People usually get married young and grow old together. It's a good system because ageing is such a gradual process that neither partner realizes until it's too late that they've married a wrinkly. Plus the wedding pictures look so much better with a fresh-faced young couple rather than a pair of old crones who need bridesmaids and a best man just to help them up the church steps.

Did you hear about the man of 86 who married a woman of 79? They spent their honeymoon getting out of the car.

∞

An 80-year-old man is going through passport control at the airport when he is pulled over by a customs official for a random search. "Excuse me, sir," says the official, "do you mind telling me how old you are?" "I'm 40," says the man. "But," says the official, "according to the date on your passport, sir, you're 80 years old." "Yes," says the old man, "but I was married for 40 years of that and you don't call that living, do you?"

∞

A middle-aged couple are walking along the beach one day when the wife points out a little old man and a little old lady walking together. "Look at those two," she says. "They look like a really happily married couple." "Maybe," says the husband. "But on the other hand they might be pointing at us and saying exactly the same thing."

∞

An old couple are arguing one day. "I don't know why I married you!" says the old woman. "Six other men proposed to me, you know." "*Six* other men!" says her husband. "You should have just married the first idiot who asked you." "I did!" says the wife. "The other six proposed afterwards."

A middle-aged woman tells her husband, "Let's go out and have some fun tonight." "Good idea!" says her husband. "But if you get home before I do, leave the hall light on."

An ageing couple are arguing. "Before we got married," yells the husband, "you told me you were oversexed." "No, I didn't!" shouts the wife. "I said I was over sex."

An ageing woman asks her husband, "Will you still love me when I'm old and ugly?" He replies without thinking, "Of course I do."

A woman tells her friend, "Last week my husband turned sixty." "So what are you going to do?" asks her friend. "I'm going to see if I can swap him for three twenties," says the woman.

∞

Two middle-aged women are talking about their marriages. "I wonder," says the first, "if my husband will still love me when my hair is grey." "Why the hell not?" says her friend. "After all, he's loved you through three shades already."

∞

An old man and his wife are having one of their many arguments. The husband says, "You remember when we got married, you promised to love, honour and obey me!" "I know," replies the wife. "But I didn't want to start an argument in front of all my friends and family, did I?"

∞

A reporter goes to visit an ageing Native American and his wife. The reporter asks the old man the name of his wife. "My wife's name," he says, "is Three

Horses." "That's a good Native American name, isn't it?" says the reporter. "Presumably when she was born her father saw three horses." "No," says the old man, "it's because all she does is Nag, Nag, Nag."

∞

A husband and wife are at a party chatting with some friends when the subject of marriage counselling comes up. "Oh, we'll never need that. My husband and I have a great relationship," says the wife. "My husband worked in communications all his life and I worked in the theatre. So he communicates really well and I just act like I'm listening."

∞

I'd rather have two girls at 21 each, than one girl at 42.

W. C. Fields

∞

An old couple are on the underground during the rush hour with everyone squeezed into the carriage when a beautiful and voluptuous young woman gets on and stands directly in front of the husband. When she gets out at the next stop she has her bottom pinched and turns round to see the old man smiling at her. "You disgusting old man!" she screams. "How dare you pinch my bottom? You ought to be ashamed of yourself at your age!" The old man looks to his wife for support. "I didn't do it!" he protests. "Honestly, I didn't touch her." "I know," says the wife, "*I* did!"

∞

An elderly couple stood before a judge following a lengthy divorce hearing. The judge addressed the woman who was 75, "So, after 50 years of marriage, love, tears, babies, grandchildren, birthdays, sicknesses and joys, why do you want to divorce your husband now?" The old woman looked first at her husband, then at the judge and slowly replied, "Because... ENOUGH IS ENOUGH!"

∞

An old man is reading a newspaper article about a scientific study into how much men and women speak during the day. "Look at this!" says the old man triumphantly to his wife. "Apparently the average woman says 30,000 words a day while the average man only says about 15,000." "Well you know why that is, don't you?" says his wife. "That's because the average woman has to repeat everything she says to the average man." The old man has carried on reading but after a moment looks up and says, "Sorry. What?"

∽

A little old man and a little old lady are celebrating having been happily married for 60 years. A newspaper reporter goes to ask them about their secret after such a long time together without ever having a cross word. "Well," says the little old husband, "it all dates back to our honeymoon in the USA 60 years ago. While we were there we visited the Grand Canyon, in Arizona, and took a trip right down to the bottom on horseback. We hadn't gone too far when my wife's horse stumbled and she almost fell off. My wife looked down at the horse and quietly said, 'That's once.' We proceeded a little further and her horse stumbled again. Again my wife quietly said, 'That's twice.' We hadn't gone a half-mile further when the horse stumbled for the third time. My wife then very quietly and calmly took out a revolver from her bag and shot the horse dead. I looked at her and yelled, 'WHAT THE HELL DO

YOU THINK YOU'RE DOING, WOMAN! WHAT'S THE YYYYING MATTER WITH YOU! YOU'VE JUST SHOT THE POOR YYYYING HORSE!!!!' And my wife looked at me and very quietly and calmly said, 'That's once.' ...And from that moment on, we've lived happily every after."

∞

An old man is invited over for dinner with a similarly aged couple. While he is there he is impressed by the way the husband precedes everything he says to his wife with endearing terms. Despite his age he constantly calls his wife "dear", "darling", "my love", "sweetness" or "beautiful". When the wife is out of the room for a few minutes, the elderly man says to the husband, "I think this is wonderful. You've been married for seventy years and yet you're still very much in love." "Why do you say that?" asks the husband. "Well," says the visitor, "because of all the pet names you keep calling your wife." The old man checks the door and then says in a whisper, "To be honest with you, I forgot what her name is about ten years ago."

∞

At the age of 60, after nearly 40 years of marriage Sid suddenly says to his wife Margaret, "I think we should divorce." "Divorce?" says Margaret. "But we've been through everything together. We're a team. Remember when you had that car accident and I nursed you back to health; when you had your drink problem and I helped you get through it; then you had those business problems and I helped support you through your bankruptcy; and then last year when the house began to subside and we had to move. Not to mention all those minor illnesses I've nursed you through." "I know," says Graham, "that's just what I mean. I've finally realized you're a jinx!"

∞

A middle-aged woman wakes up in the night and discovers that her husband is not in bed with her. She puts on her dressing gown and goes downstairs to look for him. Downstairs she sees the kitchen light on and finds him sitting there at the table, sobbing over a mug of tea. "Oh dear," says the woman. "What's the matter? What are you doing down here at this time of night?" The husband looks up from his mug of tea and asks solemnly, "Do you remember 30 years ago when we were going out together when you were only 16?" The wife is moved to tears at the thought that her husband has been so affected by the thought of their courting years. "Yes, I do," she says. The husband pauses for a moment before carrying on with a quiver in his voice, "Do you remember when your dad caught us making love in the back seat of my Ford Escort?" "Oh yes, I remember," says the wife, sitting down in the chair beside him and taking his hand. "And do you remember," says the husband, "when he pulled out that gun, held it to my head and said, 'Either you marry my daughter, or I'll make sure you go to prison for 30 years for this?'" "Oh yes," says the wife. "I remember that too. So why are you crying?" "Because," says the husband, "today's the day I would have got out."

∞

An old man and woman were married for many years, even though they clearly both hated each other's guts. Whenever they had an argument the neighbours could hear them yelling and screaming at each other all through the night. The old man would shout, "When I die, I'll dig my way up and out of the grave. Then I'll come back and haunt you for the rest of your life!" The neighbours were certainly frightened by this threat and when the old man eventually died and was buried they were surprised to see his wife celebrating and having a gay old time in the local pub afterwards.

"Aren't you worried," asked the neighbours, "that your husband will do what he said and dig his way up and out of the grave, and come back to haunt you for the rest of your life?" "No," says the old woman, "I'm not worried. He can dig as much as he likes. I had them bury him lying face down."

∞

An 85-year-old man goes to have his annual check up. The doctor asks him how he's feeling. "Never better!" boasts the old man. "I've got an 18-year-old bride who's pregnant with my child! What do you think about that?" The doctor considers this for a moment, then says, "Let me tell you a story. I knew a guy who was an avid hunter. He never missed a season. But one day went out in a bit of a hurry and he accidentally grabbed his umbrella instead of his gun. When he got to the woods, he suddenly saw a grizzly bear in front of him! He raised up his umbrella, pointed it at the bear's head, squeezed the handle and do you know what happened next?" "No," said the old man. "The bear dropped dead right in front of him, shot straight through the head!" "Ah well," says the old man, "it's obvious what happened there. Someone else must have shot that bear." "Exactly," says the doctor. "Now, getting back to this child your wife is having…"

An old married couple are lying in bed one night when suddenly, out of the blue, the wife whacks her husband on the head with a rolled-up newspaper. "Ow!" says the old man. "What on earth was that for?" "It's for the past 45 years of rotten sex," says the old woman. After a moment, the husband picks up the newspaper and whacks her with it. "Ow! And what was that for?" she asks. "For knowing the difference!" says the old man.

∞

Sid and Ethel are celebrating their fiftieth wedding anniversary. Sid says to her, "Ethel, I was wondering… have you ever been unfaithful to me?" Ethel replies, "Oh Sid, why would you ask such a question now?" "I need to know," says Sid. "Well, all right," says Ethel. "Yes, there were three times…" "Three? Well, when were they?" he asks. "Well, Sid, remember when you were thirty-five years old," says Ethel, "and you really wanted to start the business on your own and no bank would give you a loan? Remember, then one day the bank manager himself came over to the house and signed the loan papers, no questions asked?" "Oh, Ethel," says her husband, "you did that for me! I respect you more than ever. So, when was number two?" "Well, Sid, remember when you had that last heart attack," says Ethel, "and you needed that very tricky operation, and no surgeon would touch you? Then remember how Dr Wilson came all the way up here, to do the surgery himself?" "I can't believe it," says Sid. "You saved my life! I couldn't have a more wonderful wife. So, when was number three?" "Well, Sid," she says, "remember that time a few years ago, when you really wanted to be president of the golf club and you were seventeen votes short...?"

An elderly man has just got married to a young woman many years his junior. The couple have decided they want to have children together but find they have difficulty conceiving. In the end the old man decides to go to the doctor to have a fertility test. The doctor tells him to take a specimen cup home, fill it and bring it back the next day. The next day the elderly man appears back at the surgery with his specimen cup still empty. "What happened?" asks the doctor. "Well," says the old man, "first, I tried with my right hand, but nothing. So then I tried with my left hand... still nothing. My wife had a go with her right hand... nothing. She tried with her left hand... nothing. She even tried with her mouth... nothing. Then we had to call my next-door neighbour in... still nothing."

The doctor is now completely stunned. "You mean," he says, "you got your neighbour in to help." "Yes, we did," says the old man, "and do you know what? Not a single one of us could get the lid off this damn cup!"

In sickness and in health...

An old man marries a young woman several decades his junior. Although they're in love and although the old fellow tries his best, the young wife is not satisfied with their lovemaking. In the end the old man goes to a psychiatrist for advice. The psychiatrist says, "Why not try this. Hire a strapping young man. While you're making love, have him wave a towel over your bodies." "A *towel*?" asks the old man. "Yes," replies the doctor. "Your wife will be able to fantasize about the young man and waving the towel will cool you down while giving the young man something to do." The old man is desperate, so he does what the psychiatrist suggests and hires a strapping young male escort, who he orders to stand waving a towel over himself and his wife during their next attempt at lovemaking. Unfortunately the wife still doesn't seem satisfied. "I've got an idea," she says to her husband. "Why don't you and the male escort swap places for a little while?" Willing to try anything, the husband and the strapping young stallion switch positions. Within a few minutes the wife is finally satisfied. "Ah ha!" says the elderly husband in triumph to the male escort. "You see! *That's* how you wave a towel!"

∽

The old farmer married an 18-year-old girl but after a month of wedded bliss he had to visit his doctor for some advice. "It's so tiring, doctor," he said, "I'm still working the farm, and when I'm out in the field and get the urge I have to run back to the house, jump into bed, and afterwards, I have to walk back to the job again. It's wearing me out." "Well, no wonder," said the doctor. "You're 82 and she's only 18. She should be running to you." The doctor's solution to the problem was to suggest that the farmer take a shotgun out into the field, and every time he got the urge he could fire a shot to signal that his young wife should come running. A month later the doctor bumped into the old man down the high street and out of curiosity asked him how the shotgun scheme was working. "Oh, it worked very well for the first couple of weeks," said the old farmer, "but then the duck season started and I haven't seen her since."

∽

An 85-year-old man marries a beautiful and vivacious 20-year-old. Because her new husband is so old and she is worried he may over-exert himself, the woman decides that on their wedding night they should have separate bedrooms. After the festivities she prepares herself for bed and for the expected knock on the door. Sure enough, the knock comes and there is the old man all ready for action. The marriage is successfully consummated and the old man goes back to his own room and she lies down to go to sleep for the night. After a few minutes there's a knock on the door and there's the old man ready for action once more. The woman is somewhat surprised but goes along with it all once more, after which the octogenarian again bids her good night and goes back to his own room. Now the woman is really ready for a good night's sleep. She's just dropping off when unbelievably there's another knock on the door and there is her aged husband ready for action yet again. Not wanting to disappoint him, she once again succumbs to his desires. Afterwards as he is taking his leave and preparing to go back to his own room for the third time that night, she says to him, "I must say I'm really impressed that a man of your age has enough energy to do that three times in one night. I've known men less than half your age who couldn't do that. You really are a great lover." At which point her 85-year-old husband looks at her and asks, "*What*? Was I already here?"

You Know You're Getting Old When...

You can go bowling without drinking.

You can hide a spare house key in a wrinkle.

You can no longer remember your true hair colour (unless grey is the answer you're looking for).

You can remember seeing adverts for brands of cigarettes which were recommended by doctors.

You can remember when you didn't have to call the bank before you called the plumber.

You can sing and brush your teeth at the same time.

You can't tell the difference between a heart attack and an orgasm.

You can't understand all the high-tech new-fangled gadgets they have nowadays... like flush toilets.

You chat to your friends about "good grass", but you're talking about your lawns.

You confuse having a clear conscience with having a bad memory.

You daughter says she got pierced and you look at her ears.

You dim the lights for economy, not romance.

You discover that all your favourite films have been re-released in colour.

You discover the words, "whippersnapper", "scallywag" and "by crikey" creeping into your vocabulary.

You don't care where your wife goes, just so long as you don't have to go there with her.

You don't get satellite TV for the porn, you get it for the weather channel.

You don't remember being absent-minded.

You feel you can get away with a combination of black socks and sandals.

You finally reach the top of the ladder, and you find it's leaning against the wrong wall.

You find you can live without sex, but not without
your glasses.

Wise old words

A young lawyer is trying a complicated fraud case and
is constantly frustrated by the judge's interjections
and directions for the jury to ignore certain evidence
the ambitious legal eagle is putting forward. Suddenly
the young lawyer turns to the judge and says, "Your
honour, what would you do if I called you a stupid old
twit who's way past his sell-by date?" "Why, young
man," says the judge, "I'd seek to have you suspended
as being in contempt of this court and I'd do my
utmost to see that you never practised law again."
"And what if I only *thought* that you were a stupid
old twit who was way past his sell-by date?" asks the
lawyer. "If you only thought it, young man," says the
judge, "then unfortunately there would be nothing I
could feasibly do about it." "OK!" says the lawyer. "In
that case… I think you're a stupid old twit who's way
past his sell-by date."

Old Sid is sitting at his usual table in the pub taking his time over half a pint of stout. He goes to the bar halfway through the evening to order another when a well-dressed man gets the landlord's attention first. "I'll have two crates of lager, please," says the man. "And a crate of cider, and a crate of bottled beer, a dozen bottles of red wine and a dozen bottles of white..." Old Sid rattles his change around to catch the landlord's attention but the man continues, "...A bottle of whisky, a bottle of vodka and a bottle of gin please..." Sid bangs on the counter but the landlord ignores him while he continues to take the other man's order. "...a dozen bottles of tonic, a dozen bitter lemon and a couple of dozen bottles of mineral water..." Sid bangs on the bar again, but the man carries on, "...Oh, and 15 packets of peanuts, and a couple of dozen assorted packets of crisps. And what the heck, I'll have a couple of bottles of champagne as well." By this time Sid is seething, and when the man has gone he orders his half pint of stout. "I tell you what," says Sid, "You're going to go out of business the way you're carrying on." "Why do you say that?" asks the landlord. "Because," says Sid, "I'm here every bloomin' night while that flash git only comes in once a week."

∞

An ageing priest's parishioners organize a retirement dinner for him after his many years of service. The local Member of Parliament is to give a short speech before making the evening's formal presentation but unfortunately he gets held up on the way. In the MP's absence the priest decides to say a few words. "I got my first impression of this parish," he tells his parishioners, "from the very first confession I heard when I arrived here and I thought the bishop had sent me to a terrible place. The first person who came into my confessional told me he had stolen a television set and, when stopped by the police, had almost murdered the officer. He had stolen money from his parents, embezzled from his place of business, had an affair with his boss's wife and taken illegal drugs. I was horrified but as the days went on, I knew that not all my congregation were like this miscreant and that I had, indeed, come to a fine parish, full of good and loving people." Just as the priest finishes speaking the MP walks in and apologizes for being late. He immediately steps up to make his speech and begins by saying, "I'll never forget the first day our parish priest arrived. In fact, I had the honour of being the first person here to go to him for confession."

After working on the railways for 50 years, old Bill is finally retiring. The train company he works for asks him what he would like for his retirement present and Bill says he'd like his very own rail carriage, which he can keep in the back garden. The carriage would serve as his very own private hideaway, in which he could sit and think back on all the years he worked on the railways. So, to honour their most loyal employee, the train company gives Bill his very own luxury carriage and positions it just as he wants in his back garden. A year later, Bill's former boss calls by to see how he's getting on. Bill's wife answers the door and takes him through to the back garden. There, the boss is rather surprised to find Bill sitting in a seat next to his carriage smoking his pipe despite the fact that it's pouring with rain. "What are you doing?" asks the boss. "Why are you sitting out here in the rain when you could sit inside that beautiful luxury carriage we gave you?" "I've got no choice," says old Bill. "You gave me a non-smoker."

Not a prayer...

Some parents are so desperate to get their children into the right schools that they actually lie about their religion to get the place they want. Similarly, some people start going to church more when they're older to make sure they get into Heaven. When someone was surprised to find W.C. Fields reading the Bible and asked him what he was doing, he replied, "Looking for loopholes." So, religion for some people seems to be a means to an end and for others it's the meaning to The End. But in the meantime while we're down here on Earth, trying to find the punch line to the great cosmic joke, let's not forget that some of the best jokes ever uttered were about religion.

∞

An old Jewish man is very ill and in his final hours he asks for a Catholic priest to be called to his bedside. His family are very confused by this but they call for the priest anyway. "Now my son," said the priest, "I have been told you are Jewish, so why have you called for me?" "I want to convert," says the man. "But why, at this late stage in your life?" asks the priest. The old man replies, "If someone's going to die, I think it's better that it's one of your lot than one of ours."

∞

The old person's prayer: God, grant me the senility to forget the people I never liked anyway, the good fortune to run into the ones I do, and the eyesight to tell the difference.

∽

The Devil walks into a crowded bar. When the people see who it is, they all run out except for one old man. So the Devil walks up to him and says, "Do you know who I am?" The old man slowly sips his beer and answers, "Yes, I do." The Devil says, "Well then, why aren't you afraid of me?" The old man looks the Devil over and says, "Why the hell should I be scared? I've been married to your sister for 38 years."

∽

The air conditioning in a Catholic church breaks down, so they have to hire a man to crawl around in the ducts and fix whatever has broken. As the man peeks down through one of the vents in the sanctuary, he sees the elderly Mrs Murphy kneeling and saying her prayers in front of a statue of the Virgin Mary. The repairman decides to have some fun with the old lady and calls down to her, "Old lady! Old lady! This is Jesus! I tell thee thy prayers will be answered!" The little old lady doesn't even blink so the repairman presumes she can't have heard him. "This is Jesus here," he says, a little more loudly. "The Son of God! I tell thee thy prayers will be answered!" But again the little old lady doesn't answer. So the repairman tries one last time and yells at the top of his voice, "HELLO THERE, OLD LADY! THIS IS JESUS CHRIST, THE SON OF GOD! YOUR PRAYERS WILL BE ANSWERED!" At which point the little old lady looks up and says very crossly, "WILL YOU JUST SHUT UP! I'M TRYING TO TALK TO YOUR MOTHER HERE!"

∽

A pious old man reaches the age of 100 and suddenly stops going to church. The priest is alarmed that the old fellow has suddenly decided not to come to the services any more so he goes to visit him at home. He finds the old man in perfect health and completely mobile. So the priest asks, "Why is it we never see you in church any more?" "Well, I'll tell you, father," says the old man. "I got to be 80 and I thought God would take me any day. Then I got to be 85, then 90, then 95. Now I'm 100 years old and I reckon God must have forgotten me. So I'd better not go and remind him I'm still here."

∽

A little old lady who is a devout Christian lives next door to a young man who is an equally devout atheist. Every morning the lady comes out onto her front step and exclaims, "Praise the Lord for the new morning!" Every morning the atheist next door shouts back to her, "Shut up, you old fool! There is no God!" Every morning the same exchange happens. As time goes on, the lady runs into financial difficulties and has trouble buying food. One morning she goes out onto her front step and prays aloud to God for help with her groceries, before finishing with her usual, "Praise the Lord!" The next morning she opens her door and is astounded to find a bag full of groceries sitting there, waiting for her. Her response is of course, "Praise the Lord for he has provided me with groceries!" At this moment the atheist jumps up from behind her garden wall and says, "Ha, I got you! It was me that bought you those groceries. You see, there is no God!" The little old lady looks at him for a moment and then cries, "Praise the Lord, not only did you get me my groceries, oh Lord, you got Satan to pay for them!"

∞

An old lady is talking to her parish priest. The priest tells her that at her time of life, she should be giving some thought to what he calls "the hereafter". "Oh

I already think about that all the time," she tells him. "You *do*?" says the priest, surprised. "Oh yes," she says, "whenever I go into a room or open a drawer or wardrobe I always have to think to myself, 'Now then, what was it I'm here after?'"

∞

An old man was sitting on his porch one day watching the rain come down. Soon the water was lapping over the porch and into the old man's house and still he sat there watching it. A rescue boat came by and the people on board told him, "You can't stay there. You'll have to come with us." "No, don't worry," the old man told them, "God will save me." The boat moved on and the rain kept coming down until it was lapping up the old man's stairs. Another rescue boat appeared and the people on board again told the old man he had to come with them. "No, don't worry," said the old man again. "God will save me." So the boat left and the rain carried on coming down until the old man was left sitting on his roof, surrounded by water. This time a rescue helicopter appeared and told the old man to climb aboard but again he said, "No, don't worry. God will save me." So the helicopter flew off and the water kept rising until the old man was swept away and drowned. When he arrives in Heaven, the old man tells God, "I placed my faith in you but you did nothing to save me." "What do you mean, I did nothing?" says God, "I sent you two boats and a bloody helicopter!"

∞

One day a post-office sorting worker finds a letter that has arrived addressed to God. He opens it and reads: "Dear God, I hope you can help me. Last Thursday I was mugged and had my purse stolen. In it was £50 which I had been saving for a toy for my great-grandson's birthday. It has really upset me that I won't be able to buy it. I am crying as I write this letter. Please help if you can. Yours faithfully, Ethel Higginbotham, aged 83." The letter is shown round the staff in the sorting office and the workers are all touched by the sad story. Being generous souls they decide to have a whip round for the old lady and they raise £46. They put the money in an envelope and send it back to Ethel. One week later another letter turns up addressed to God. The staff gather round eagerly as the letter is opened: "Dear God," says the letter, "I can't thank you enough. I bought my grandson his present and his little face lit up and we had a wonderful day – thank you, Lord. Yours

faithfully, Ethel. P.S. When I opened your letter
I noticed it was £4 short. I expect it was those
thieving bastards at the Post Office!"

∞

Old Matilda was well known at her local church
as the town gossip and self-appointed monitor of
morals in her neighbourhood, forever sticking her
nose into other people's business. Many of the other
members of the church congregation did not approve
of her activities, but feared her enough to maintain
their silence. She made a mistake, however, when she
accused Bert, another elderly churchgoer, of being an
alcoholic after she saw his bright orange P Reg Skoda
parked in front of the local pub one afternoon. She
told Bert and everyone else within earshot that anyone
seeing his car there would immediately recognize it
and know just what he was doing. Bert, a man of
few words, stared at her for a moment and then just
turned and walked away. He didn't explain, defend
or deny; he said nothing. Later that evening however,
Bert quietly parked his bright orange P Reg Skoda
in front of Mildred's house and then walked home,
leaving the car there all night.

Never too late to woo

An old man and an old lady have been good friends for many years. Finally one day the old man decides he will ask the old lady out for dinner one night and request her hand in marriage. "Oh yes," says the old lady, as she tucks into her dessert. Later, the pair go home to their respective houses. When the old man wakes up the next morning the events of the previous evening are a little hazy and he is unable to remember whether his lady friend said yes or no to the offer of marriage. After fretting about this all morning, he decides he will have to phone and ask her. "This is rather embarrassing," he says. "Last night I asked you to marry me but now I'm afraid I can't remember what you said." "Oh, I said yes," says the old lady, "but I'm glad you called because, to be honest with you, I woke up this morning and couldn't remember who it was who had asked me."

An elderly couple are watching an evangelist on television one night. The preacher faces the camera and announces, "My friends, I'd like to share my healing powers with everyone watching this programme. Place one hand on top of your television set and the other hand on the part of your body which ails you and lo, I will heal thee!" The old woman has been having terrible stomach problems, so she places one hand on the television, and her other hand on her stomach. Meanwhile, her husband approaches the television, placing one hand on top of the TV and his other hand on his groin. With a frown his wife tells him, "Ernest, the man is healing the sick, not raising the bloody dead!"

The dating game

A doctor gets a visit from an old man. "I seem to have a terrible problem whenever I have sex, doctor," he says. "The last time I had sex with my wife I felt terribly hot and sweaty, but the time before that it was completely the opposite. I felt terribly cold and shivery." "Oh dear," says the doctor. "This sounds as though you may have a serious condition. I'd better have a word with your wife." So the doctor goes to see the old man's wife and tells her all about the symptoms her husband has been suffering. "Oh, the stupid old fool!" says the old lady. "Do you know what might be causing the problem then?" asks the doctor. "I certainly do," says the old woman. "We only have sex twice a year. Last time it was in the middle of July and the time before that it was the middle of winter."

∞

A couple in their seventies go to a private doctor's surgery. "OK," says the doctor. "What can I do for you?" The old man says, "Will you watch us have sexual intercourse?" The doctor is rather puzzled, but agrees. When the couple have finished, the doctor says, "Well, I can't see any particular problem there. And of course as this is a private practice I'm going to have to charge you £25 for the consultation." The couple pay up, but a week later they're back asking for the doctor to watch them having sex once again. Again he can't see any particular problem and charges them £25. When they turn up for the third week in a row, the doctor asks them, "Just what exactly are you trying to find out?" "We're not trying to find out anything," says the old man. "She is married to someone else so we can't go to her house. I'm married so we can't go to my house. The only hotel round here charges £75. Here, it only costs £25 which, because I'm a pensioner, I can claim back from the NHS."

∞

Two ageing widows are talking to one another. The first says, "That nice George Johnson asked me out for a date. I know you went out with him last week, and I wanted to talk with you about him before I give him my answer." "Well," says the second, "I'll tell you about him. He showed up at my house right on time at seven o'clock. He was dressed very smartly in his suit and tie and he brought me a lovely bunch of flowers! Then he took me downstairs and showed me into a beautiful Rolls-Royce complete with uniformed chauffeur. Then he took me out for a wonderful dinner at the finest restaurant in town. We had lobster, champagne, dessert and a bottle of vintage wine. Afterwards we went to the theatre and enjoyed the show immensely but then on the way back home, I could hardly believe it. He turned into an ANIMAL. He went completely berserk and started tearing off my expensive new dress in his desperate desire to get his hands on my body and ravish me." "Oh my goodness," says the old lady's friend. "So you're telling me you don't think I should go out with him?" "No," says the first old lady, "I'm telling you that when you go out with him, remember to wear an old dress."

∞

A coach driver is taking a group of old people on a day trip. An old lady appears from the back of the bus and tells him that she has just been molested. "Don't be ridiculous," says the coach driver. "Who would have molested you on this trip?" A few miles further on, another old lady totters to the front of the bus and tells him she has also been molested. "What's the matter with you?" says the driver. "You must all be senile." But after a third old lady comes forward to say that she too has just been molested, the driver thinks he had better stop and investigate. At the back of the bus he finds an old man crawling round on his hands and knees under the seats. "What do you think you're doing?" asks the driver. "I've dropped my toupee," says the old man. "Three times now I thought I'd found it, but when I tried to grab it, it ran off."

∞

A little old lady is in court describing what happened during a particularly shocking recent crime in a local park. "Please tell the court," says the lawyer, "what happened when the young man sat down next to you on the park bench." "He started rubbing my thigh," says the little old lady. "And were the police called at this point?" asks the lawyer.

"No," replies the old lady. "Please tell the court what happened next," asks the lawyer. "Then he started to fondle my bosoms," says the little old lady. "I see," says the lawyer, "and was this when the police became involved?" "No," says the little old lady. "Then please tell the court what happened after that," asks the lawyer. "That's when he started kissing me and suggested we go into the bushes for a bit of you know what," says the little old lady. "I see," says the lawyer. "And is that when the police were called to the scene?" "No," replies the old lady. "In that case, madam," says the lawyer. "Please could you tell the court at exactly what stage the police were called to the scene." And the old lady replies, "When he shouted 'April fool!' and I got out my gun and shot the teasing bastard!"

An old couple have been married for 50 years. One morning they are sitting at the breakfast table when the old gentleman says, "Just think, my darling, we've been married for 50 years. Remember all the passion we used to have for each other. When we were first married we used to wander round the house naked as nature intended." "Well, why shouldn't we do the same now?" asks his wife and strips off her clothes right there at the breakfast table. "What are you doing, woman?" says the old man. "What if someone comes to the door?" "Come on!" says the old woman, leaning across the table. "Where's your passion gone? Doesn't the sight of me naked stir anything in you? You know I've got a warm feeling in my breasts for you right now." "I'm not surprised," says her husband, "you've just dipped one of them in your coffee and the other in your porridge."

∞

An old lady is upset because her ageing husband is no longer able to satisfy her physical needs. She visits the doctor to ask for advice. The doctor gives her a prescription for Viagra and tells him to put three drops in his milk before he goes to bed. A couple of weeks later, the woman returns. The doctor asks if the Viagra was effective. "I'm afraid not," says the old lady. "I put 30 drops in his milk by accident. Now my husband has died and I've had to come to you for the antidote." "Why do you need an antidote if he's already dead?" asks the doctor. "Because," says the old lady, "how else am I going to be able to get the lid down on his coffin?"

∞

An 80-year-old man goes to the doctor for a check-up. The doctor is amazed at what good shape the guy is in and tells him, "You're doing incredibly well for a man of your age. Tell me, how old was your dad when he died?" "Who said my dad's dead?" says the old man. The doctor is amazed. "You mean you're 80 years old and your dad's still alive? How old is he?" "He's 100 years old," says the old man. "How extraordinary," says the doctor, "How about your dad's dad? How old was he when he died?" "Who said my granddad's dead?" says the old man. The doctor is stunned. "You mean you're 80 years old," he says, "and your grandfather's still living? How old is he?" "He's 118," says the old man. "In fact he got married just the other week." "*Married*!" exclaims the doctor. "Why would a 118-year-old man want to get married?" "Who said he wanted to?" says the old man.

∞

An old man is celebrating his 115th birthday and the local newspaper sends a reporter round to interview him. The reporter notices the old man's house and garden are full of children of all ages playing together. A beautiful young girl aged about 19 answers the door and shows the reporter in. The reporter asks the old man, "So all these youngsters must be your grandchildren." "Oh no," says the old man. "They're all mine." "All of them?" asks the reporter. "Of course," says the old man. "Including the beautiful young woman who showed me in?" asks the reporter. "Oh no, not her," says the old man, "she's my wife." "Your wife?" says the surprised reporter. "But she can't be more than 19 years old." "That's right." says the old man with pride. "But I would have thought it would be difficult for you to have much of a sex life, what with you being 115 and your wife being a teenager." "Are you joking or what?" says the old man. "We have sex every single night. Every night two of my boys help me on top and every morning six of my boys help me off again." "Hang on," says the reporter, "Why does it take only two of your boys to put you on, but it takes six of them to get you off?" "Well, it wouldn't take so many," says the old man, "but I keep putting up a fight."

∞

An old man goes into his doctor's surgery saying that he feels tired. "Have you been doing anything unusual recently?" asks the doctor. "Well," says the old man, "Wednesday night I picked up a 20-year-old girl and we had sex five times. Thursday night, I picked up a 19-year-old and we had sex eight times and then last night I picked up a pair of 18-year-old twins and we had sex twenty times." "My goodness," says the doctor. "No wonder you're feeling tired. I hope you took precautions with these women." "I certainly did," says the old man, "I gave them all a false name."

The cheek of it

An old man comes out of the newsagents and crosses over to the car parked opposite, where a traffic warden is writing a ticket. "Oh come on!" says the old man. "I'm a pensioner. I can't afford to pay that, can I?" The traffic warden ignores him and continues writing out the ticket. The old man becomes more abusive. "You fascist!" he says. "You slimy piece of I don't know what! You've got no heart. You pathetic, jumped-up stupid little man!" The traffic warden proceeds to write out another ticket and then another as the old man keeps ranting on at him about his lack of consideration. The car ends up with five tickets on the windscreen. "You should have spoken to him a bit more nicely," says a passer-by to the old man, "and then he might have let you off." "I don't care," says the old man. "This isn't my car."

∽

An old Jewish man is making a long-distance call in the USA when all of a sudden he gets cut off. He hollers, "Operator, giff me beck da party!" She says, "I'm sorry, sir, you'll have to make the call all over again." He says, "What do you want from my life? Giff me beck da party." "I'm sorry, sir," says the operator, "you'll have to place the call again." "Operator, ya know vat?" says the old man. "You can take da telephone and shove it in you-know-vere!" And with that he hangs up. Two days later he opens the door and there are two big, strapping men standing in his way telling him, "We came to take your telephone away." "Vy?" asks the old man. "Because," they say, "two days ago you insulted Operator number 28. But if you'd like to call up and apologize, we'll leave the telephone here." "Vait a minute," says the old man, "vat's da rush? Vat's da hurry?" He goes to the telephone and dials. "Hello? Get me Operator 28. Hello, Operator 28? Remember me? Two days ago I insulted you? I told you to take da telephone and shove it in you-know-vere?" "Yes?" says the operator. "Vell," he says, "get ready... they're bringin' it to ya now!"

∞

An old lady from a remote village in Cornwall goes to stay with her niece in Surrey. Nearby is a very well-known golf course. On the second afternoon of her visit, the elderly lady goes for a walk. Upon her return, her niece asks, "Well, Auntie, did you enjoy yourself?" "Oh, yes, indeed," says the old lady. "Before I had walked very far, I came to some beautiful rolling fields. There seemed to be a number of people wandering around them, mostly men. Some of them kept shouting at me in a very eccentric manner, but I took no notice. There were four men who followed me for some time, uttering curious excited barking sounds. Naturally, I ignored them, too. Oh, by the way," she says, holding out her hands, "I found a number of these curious little round white balls, so I picked them all up and brought them home hoping you could explain what they're all about."

Sticky situations

Two guys left the bar after a long night of drinking, jumped in the car and started it up. After a couple of minutes, an old man appeared in the passenger window and tapped lightly. The passenger screamed, "Look at the window. There's an old ghost's face there!" The driver sped up, but the old man's face stayed in the window. The passenger rolled his window down part way and, scared out of his wits, said, "What do you want?" The old man softly replied, "You got any tobacco?" The passenger handed the old man a cigarette and yelled, "Step on it!" to the driver, while rolling up the window in terror. A few minutes later they calmed down and started laughing again. The driver said, "I don't know what happened, but don't worry: the speedometer says we're doing 80 now." All of a sudden there was a light tapping on the window and the old man reappeared. "There he is again," the passenger yelled. He rolled down the window and shakily said, "Yes?" "Do you have a light?" the old man quietly asked. The passenger threw a lighter out the window saying, "Step on it!" They were driving about 100 miles an hour, trying to forget what they had just seen and heard, when all of a sudden there came some more tapping. "Oh my God, he's back!" The passenger rolled down the window and screamed in stark terror, "WHAT DO YOU WANT WITH US?" The old man gently replied, "I just wondered if you wanted any help getting out of the mud?"

∞

An avid young golfer finds himself with a few hours to spare after work one day. He works out that if he hurries and plays as fast as he can, he could get in nine holes before he has to go home. Just as he is about to tee off, an old gentleman shuffles onto the tee and asks if he can accompany the young man as he is golfing alone. The young golfer doesn't like to refuse and lets the old gent join him. To his surprise the old man plays fairly quickly. He doesn't hit the ball far but nevertheless plods along consistently without wasting much time. Eventually they reach the ninth fairway, and the young man finds himself with a tough shot. A large pine tree stands right in the direct line of his shot, between him and the green. After several minutes of debating how to hit the shot, the old man finally tells him, "When I was your age I was able to hit the ball right over the top of that tree." With this gauntlet thrown down, the youngster swings as hard as he can and hits the ball right smack into the top of the tree trunk, where it thuds back on the ground less than a foot from where it started. "Damn it!" says the young golfer. "How on earth did you manage to hit the ball over that tree?" "Well," says the old man, "of course in those days the tree was only three feet tall…"

Things ain't what they used to be

A granddad is talking to his grandson. "How many miles do you walk to school?" asks granddad. "About half a mile," says the boy. "Huh!" snorts granddad. "When I was your age I walked eight miles to school every day. What grades did you get on your last report?" "Mostly B's," says the boy. "Huh!" says granddad in disgust. "When I was your age I was getting straight A's. Have you ever been in a fight?" "Twice," says the boy, "and got beaten up both times." "Huh!" says granddad. "When I was your age I was in a fight every day. How old are you anyway? "Nine years old," says the boy. "Huh!" snorts granddad. "When I was your age I was eleven."

An old man is telling his grandson about how he used to work in a blacksmith's when he was a boy. "Oh yes," says the old man, "I had to really toughen myself up to work in that place. Do you know I would stand at the back of my house, get a five-pound potato sack in my right hand and a five-pound potato sack in my left hand, and then raise my arms up and extend them straight out from my sides? I'd then stand there holding them out like that for as long as I could. After a while I moved onto ten-pound potato sacks, then twenty-pound potato sacks. Finally I was able to do it with a pair of fifty-pound potato sacks." "Wow," granddad," says the little boy. "That must have been hard." "Oh yes," says the old man, "it was. And it was even worse when I started putting potatoes in the sacks."

∞

Three old men are chatting about their ancestors and boasting about what they had done in the forces. The first one says, "My great grandfather was in the First World War trenches and survived." The second one says, "Well, my great grandfather was in the Boer War and he survived." Not to be outdone the third one says, "Well, if my great grandfather was alive today he'd be internationally famous." "Really?" say the other two, leaning forward. "Why's that?" "Because he'd be 153 years old," says the third old man.

Helpful helpers

An old man is finding it increasingly difficult to get around so he asks his similarly aged neighbour if he would mind popping into town to the post office to see if a package he is expecting has turned up yet. His old neighbour says he was going into town anyway to get his groceries. So off he totters, all the way down the street and into the town. The old man sits watching for several hours until eventually his elderly neighbour re-appears, slowly plodding all the way back down the street again. "So?" says the old man to his neighbour. "Was my package there?" "Oh yes," says the neighbour. "It's there all right."

An elderly spinster calls her lawyer's office and tells the receptionist she wants to see her solicitor to have her will drawn up. The receptionist suggests they set up an appointment for a convenient time for the spinster to come into the office. The woman says, "You must understand, I've lived alone all my life, I rarely see anyone and I don't like to go out. Would it be possible for the lawyer to come to my house?" The receptionist checks with one of the junior partners and he agrees to visit the old lady at home to draw up her will. The young solicitor's first question is, "Could you tell me what you have in assets and how you'd like them to be distributed under your will?" The old lady says, "Besides the furniture and accessories you see here,

I have £40,000 in my savings account at the bank."
"Tell me," the solicitor asks, "how would you like
the £40,000 to be distributed?" The old lady says,
"Well, as I've told you, I've lived a reclusive life,
people have hardly ever noticed me, so I'd like them
to notice me after I've passed on. I'd like to provide
£35,000 for my funeral." "Well," says the solicitor,
"for £35,000 you will be able to have a funeral that
will certainly be noticed. It's sure to be one that
will leave a lasting impression on anyone who may
not have taken much note of you before! But tell
me, what would you like to do with the remaining
£5,000?" "Well, as you know," says the spinster,
"I've never married, I've lived alone almost my
entire life, and in fact I've never slept with a man.
I'd like you to use the £5,000 to arrange for a man
to sleep with me." "This is a very unusual request,"
the solicitor says, "but I'll make some enquiries
and see what I can do to arrange it for you." That
evening, the young solicitor tells his wife about the
eccentric old spinster and her strange request. After
thinking about how much she could do around
the house with £5,000, and with a bit of coaxing,
she persuades her husband to agree to provide
the service himself. She says, "I'll drive you over
tomorrow morning, and wait in the car until you're
finished." The next morning, she drives him to the

spinster's house and waits while he goes into the house. She sits waiting for over an hour, but still her husband doesn't come out. In the end, in frustration she sounds the car horn to hurry her husband up. A few moments later, the upstairs window opens up, the solicitor sticks his head out and yells, "Come back and pick me up this time tomorrow. She's agreed to let the council bury her!"

Death and the afterlife

An old man lying on his deathbed summons his doctor, his lawyer and his priest. He hands out three separate envelopes to them. Each of the envelopes contains £30,000. "Gentlemen," he tells them solemnly, "they say you can't take it with you but I am going to try. When they lower my coffin into my grave, I want each of you to throw in these envelopes I have just given you." After the funeral the doctor confesses to the other two, "I've got to be straight with you. My health practice desperately needed some money to build a new clinic, so I kept £20,000 and just threw in £10,000." The priest also confesses, "The church is in desperate need of renovation, so I'm afraid I kept £10,000 and just threw in £20,000." The lawyer stands there, shaking his head in disgust. "I can't believe you two," he says. "Am I the only one of us who was decent enough to carry out the old man's dying wishes?" "So you threw in the entire £30,000!" say the doctor and the priest in astonishment. "Yes," says the lawyer. "Well… I threw in a cheque for the full amount."

✎

Joe tells his friend Pete, "My granddad died last night." "Oh no," says Pete. "Yes," says Joe, "he was working late in the whisky distillery, he had to climb up to check in one of the vats but being a bit doddery on his legs now he lost his balance and fell in." "Oh my goodness!" says Pete. "So what happened? Did he drown?" "Yes, after eight hours," says Joe. "Eight hours!" says Pete. "Why so long?" "Well, it would have been quicker," says Joe, "but he had to get out three times to go to the toilet."

✎

An old man asks his wife, "Darling, if I died, would you ever consider getting married again?" "I've no idea!" says his wife. "But maybe after a considerable period of grieving, I might consider it. After all, we all need companionship." "OK," says the old man, "but if I died and you got married again, would your new husband live in this house?" "I've no idea!" says his wife. "But then again we've spent a lot of money getting this house the way we want it. I'm not going to get rid of it easily, so perhaps he would." "OK," says the old man, "and if I died and you got married again and your new husband came to live in this house, would he sleep in our bed?" "I've no idea!" says his wife. "But then again I suppose this bed is brand new and it cost us £2,000. It's going to last a long time, so maybe." "OK," says the old man, "and if I died and you got married again, and he came to live in this house and slept in our bed, would you let him use my golf clubs?" "Oh no," says his wife. "He's left-handed!"

∞

An old Jewish woman goes to a travel agent and asks for a holiday in Calcutta because she wants to consult with the Indian mystics. "Oh, it won't be very suitable for a woman of your age," says the travel agent, "How about a nice cruise?" But the woman insists and takes the trip to Calcutta. When she gets there it's very hot and there are flies buzzing round her as she comes out of the airport and boards a ramshackle old bus. She is on the bus for several uncomfortable hours and finally reaches a remote spot, where there is a temple. There is a queue of people waiting to see the guru so she waits and waits and waits until finally she is allowed in. "Now remember," says one of the men at the door of the temple, "You are only permitted to utter five words to the guru." The woman nods and goes in to where the guru sits in a dark corner. She approaches him and says, "Albie, come home right now!"

∞

An old miser is on his death bed. He's been hoarding his cash for years and he thinks he's found a way of taking it with him. He instructs his housekeeper to cash a large cheque then take the money and stuff it into two pillowcases. Once the cases are stuffed with notes the housekeeper is told to hide them in the attic. The housekeeper does as she's asked, but can't understand what the old man is up to. The miser explains his idea to her, "When I die, I'll drift upwards to Heaven. On the way I'll make sure I waft up through the ceiling. Then I can grab one pillowcase in each hand and take my loot to the afterlife." The housekeeper thinks this sounds a little eccentric but she says nothing. A few days later, she takes the miser his breakfast and finds him dead in his bed. After calling the doctor and the undertaker, she goes into the attic to see if the miser's plan has been successful, but it seems it hasn't. The two pillowcases are exactly where she left them. "I knew it!" she says to herself. "That old fool should have told me to put them down in the basement."

∞

An old priest dies and is waiting in line at the Pearly Gates. Ahead of him is a man dressed in sunglasses, a loud shirt, leather jacket and jeans. Saint Peter asks him, "What have you done, that I should admit you into the Kingdom of Heaven?" The man replies, "I have been a taxi driver for many years." Saint Peter consults his list. He smiles and says to the taxi driver, "Take this silken robe and golden staff, and enter the Kingdom." The taxi driver goes into Heaven with his robe and staff. Next, it's the priest's turn. He stands erect and booms out, "I have been a priest for the last forty years." Saint Peter consults his list. He says to the priest, "Take this cotton robe and wooden staff, and enter the Kingdom." "Just a minute," says the priest. "That man was a taxi driver and he gets a silken robe and golden staff. How can this be?" "Up here, we work by results," says Saint

Peter. "While you preached, people slept; while he drove, people prayed."

∞

After losing her husband a woman decides to try and contact him through a medium. After a while the medium says she thinks the husband is with them. "How are you?" the widow asks. "I'm fine," says the husband, "In fact, I'm great. I'm in a lovely green field surrounded by cows." "Oh," says the widow, rather surprised. "And some of them are very attractive," says the husband. "Really?" says the widow, "And are there angels there?" "No, just cows," says the husband. "I think I'm going to enjoy myself." "Well, that's good, I suppose," said the widow, "But why do you keep going on about cows?" "Didn't I tell you?" says the husband, "I'm on a farm at Ilkley Moor – I've come back as a bull."

∞

A young man is building a brick wall outside his house one day when a man stops to congratulate him. "What a magnificent wall you've built, young man, I doubt whether even Cornelius Bagshot III could have built a wall as good as that." "Who?" asks the young man. "Cornelius Bagshot III," says the passer-by. "He was an incredible man. He could do anything he set his mind to: an outstanding athlete, leading light of Mensa, a chess grandmaster, a brilliant footballer and cricketer and mountain climber. And he was an incredible lover as well, by all accounts. He knew exactly what women wanted in the bedroom department, if you know what I mean. He was certainly an incredible, brilliant man, the like of whom we will not see again." "So was he a friend of yours then, this Cornelius Bagshot III?" asks the young man. "No, I never met him," says the passer-by. "I just married his widow."

No fools

A little old lady walked into the head branch of a respected bank, holding a large paper bag in her hand. She told the young man at the window that she wished to take the £3 million she had in the bag and open an account with the bank. As it was such a large sum she asked to meet the manager of the bank first. The teller seemed to think that was a reasonable request and after opening the paper bag and seeing the bundles of £50 notes, which amounted to around £3 million, he telephoned the manager's secretary to arrange this. The old lady was escorted upstairs and ushered into the manager's office. Introductions were made and the lady stated that she would like to get to know the people she did business with on a more personal level. The bank manager then asked her how she came into such a large amount of money. "Was it an inheritance?" he asked. "No," she answered. "Was it from playing the stock market?" "No," she replied. He was quiet for a minute, trying to think of where this little old lady could possibly have come into £3 million. "I bet on things," she stated. "You bet?" repeated the bank manager, "as in horses?" "No," she replied, "I bet on people." Seeing his confusion, she explained that she just bet different things with people. All of a sudden she said, "I'll bet you £25,000 that by ten o'clock tomorrow morning, your balls will be square." The bank manager figured she must be off her rocker and decided to take her up on the bet. He didn't see how he could lose. For the rest of the day, the bank manager was very careful. He decided to stay home that evening and take no chances; there was £25,000 at stake. When he got up in the morning and took his shower, he checked to make sure everything was OK. There was no difference; he looked the same as he always had. He went to work and waited for the little old lady to come in at ten o'clock, humming as he went. He knew this would be a good day; how often do you get handed £25,000 for doing nothing? At ten o'clock sharp, the little old lady was shown into his office. With her was a much younger man. When he inquired as to the man's purpose for being there, she informed him that he was her lawyer and she always took him along when there was that much money involved. "Well?" she asked, "what about our bet?" "I don't know how to tell you this," he replied, "but I am the same as I've always been, only £25,000 richer." The little old lady seemed to accept this, but requested that she be able to see for herself. The bank manager thought this was reasonable and dropped his trousers. She instructed him to bend over and then grabbed hold of him. Sure enough, everything was fine. The bank manager then looked up and saw her lawyer standing across the room-banging his head against the wall. "What's wrong with him?" he inquired. "Oh, *him*!" she replied, "I bet him £100,000 that by ten o'clock this morning I'd have the bank manager by the bollocks."

Three old men are talking about what their grandchildren might be saying about them in fifty years' time. "I would like my grandchildren to say, 'He was successful in business,'" says the first old man. "Fifty years from now," says the second, "I want them to say, 'He was a loyal family man.'" Turning to the third old man, the first gent asks, "So what do you want them to say about you in fifty years?" "*Me?*" says the third old man. "I want them all to say, 'My, he looks good for his age!'"

∽

I went to the cinema the other day and in the front row was an old man and with him was his dog. It was a sad, funny kind of film – you know the type. In the sad part, the dog cried his eyes out, and in the funny part, the dog laughed his head off. This happened all the way through the film. After the film had ended, I decided to go and speak to the old man. "That's the most amazing thing I've seen," I said. "That dog really seemed to enjoy the film. It's remarkable!" "Yeah, it is," said the old man. "He hated the book."

∽

A man, 92 years old, is told by his doctor that he has tested positive for HIV. Distraught and befuddled, he retires as usual to spend the afternoon at the park bench with other senior citizens. He tells his friend: "Can you believe it? I have HIV... at 92." His friend replies, "You think you have troubles? I have IBM at 80."

∞

An old man of 87 went to the hospital to get a radical new surgical procedure done, where they stretch the skin and pull all the wrinkles up onto the top of the scalp, making you appear years younger. On his way out of the hospital, he met an old friend who didn't recognize him at first. "Rob, is that really you?" said the friend. "You look years younger! I didn't know you had a dimple in your chin." "It's not a dimple, it's my belly button," said the old man and his friend laughed. "If you think that's funny, take a look at what I'm wearing for a tie," he continued.

∞

An extremely old man visits his doctor and tells him, "I need my sex drive lowered." The doctor, incredulous, says, "What? You want your sex drive lowered?" To which the old man replies: "It's all in my head; I need it LOWERED."

∞

One sunny Sunday in spring, Father Fitzpatrick noticed that there was a smaller gathering than usual for the noon service. So as soon as the final hymn was sung, he slipped out the back way and went along the street to see who was out and about instead of coming to church. The first person he saw was old Mrs O'Neill, sitting on a park bench with her cane beside her. The good cleric sat down next to her and said, "Good afternoon, Mrs O'Neill, why weren't you in church today?" Mrs O'Neill replied: "Well, Father, it was just such a lovely day today I didn't want to be cooped up in that stuffy old church." The priest was a bit taken aback by this blunt answer, so he thought for a minute, then asked, "But Mrs O'Neill, don't you want to go to Heaven?" To his surprise, the elderly lady shook her head vehemently and said, "No, Father." At that, the priest got to his feet indignantly and said firmly, "Then I am ashamed for you." Now it was Mrs O'Neill's turn to be surprised. She looked up at him and said, "Oh, Father, I thought you meant right now."

∞

Jesus returned and ended up by the side of the River Severn in Worcestershire. He confronted an old chap who was sat there fishing. "I am Jesus – I have come to save all from the horrors that be," exclaimed the great one. "Sod off, you're scaring the fish," answered the old one. "No, you don't understand – I have returned to save the Earth, now tell me, where should I start?" The old boy thinks for a while and tells him to perform a miracle, then he will believe that this is truly The Lord. "Walk across the river," he tells Jesus. So Jesus starts walking across the river, and the water is lapping round his ankles – then around his shins, then his knees. This starts to worry him, but he continues, knowing that he can do it. The next thing he knows, he slips and disappears under the water, and nearly drowns. He manages to claw his way back to the shore, and the old man says to him: "There you are, see, you're not Jesus, you can't walk across water." Jesus responds, "Well, I used to be able to do it until I got these holes in my feet…"

Never too old for...

A bloke gives his 85-year-old father a surprise visit from a hooker as a birthday present. He answers the door, and, forewarned, she bubbles at him: "Hi, I'm here to give you super sex." He looks at her for a moment, then replies: "Um, thanks. I'll have the soup."

∞

If you reach 90, you can help advance medical science. There isn't much we know about sex at that age. Rats don't live that long...

∞

Two elderly men are sitting at the bar, watching the young girls go by. One says to the other: "You know, I'm still sexually interested in women. In fact, I always get excited when I see the young girls walking by. The real problem is that at this age, I don't see so well any more."

∞

Old age and treachery always beats youth and talent.

∞

Their respective spouses having died, a couple in their late sixties decide to marry and move to Bournemouth. In preparation for this they talk through the sharing of household expenses and various other matters. Jane asks Harold what they should do about their present houses. "Well, we ought to each sell our home and then we can each fund half the purchase price of our new home." Jane agrees. Harold then asks Jane what she'd like to do about the grocery bills. She suggests: "Neither one of us eats very much, so maybe we ought to split that bill on a monthly basis." Harold agrees. Then what about the utility bill? Again, they decide to share. Then Jane asks Harold what he wants to do about sex, to which he replies: "Oh, infrequently." Jane looks at him and asks: "Is that one word or two?"

There were these three catering students driving along an country road one day when they saw a farm. So they pulled in, and knocked on the old farmer's door. The farmer answered the door and the three students introduced themselves and said: "We were just passing by and saw your field of buttercups, and were wondering if we could go and get a bucket full of butter." The old farmer scratched his head and said: "You boys ain't gonna get no butter from buttercups, but you're more than welcome to try." About an hour later, the three came back, thanked the farmer and drove off with their bucket full of butter. The farmer once again scratched and shook his head, mumbled under his breath and went on about his business. About three months later, the same three students came up to the farm, knocked on the door and asked the old farmer if he remembered them. He chuckled and asked what he could do for them this time. One of them said: "We were just driving by and happened to see you now have a field of milkweed and we were wondering if we could go out and get a bucket of milk?" Once again, the old farmer chuckled, shook his head, scratched it and sarcastically said: "You boys go on out there and get your milk from my milkweeds." Once again, about an hour later, the three came back with their bucket overflowing with fresh milk and drove off. This time, the farmer was really confused, but just a little less sceptical. It was about three or four months later when the three agricultural students came back and again knocked on the old farmer's door, this time saying that they were driving by and saw the field full of pussywillows. This time, the old farmer went with them.

Drink and drugs

There's a bar where all the regulars are really into body-building. The owner is a body-builder and he only employs body-builders as bar staff. The walls are covered in body-builder photos and they are always having body-builder competitions. On the wall behind the bar is a sign that says, "Win €1,000: Beat The Bartender." Written below it are the rules of the competition: "The bartenders are so strong that, after any one of them has squeezed a lemon with his bare hands, nobody can ever squeeze anything else out of it: anyone who can will win the prize." The space around the bar is filled with photos of people who have tried to win the competition, but failed. One day, a skinny, sad-faced little old man walks into the bar and announces he'd like to try for the prize. It is a Saturday night, the bar is packed and everybody starts to laugh. The guy's head is about the size of the bartender's hand, and he's over 60 to boot, and nobody believes he has a chance. The bartender picks up a lemon and starts to squeeze it. The juice gushes out quickly, but after a few seconds it stops as the man squeezes everything out: juice, pips, pith and even squashed rind. The bartender then hands the lemon husk to the tiny old man. The man puts his hand around

the wizened, almost unrecognizable lemon and
starts to squeeze. To the astonishment of everyone
present, juice begins to drip from the fruit and
before long seven, eight, nine, and then ten full
drops have been squeezed! Everyone starts to cheer
and the bartender coughs up the money. "That's
amazing – really amazing," says the bartender. "Are
you a secret body-builder? Are you a martial arts
expert? How did you do it?" "That was quite easy
actually," says the old man, looking modest. "I work
for the Inland Revenue."

∽

An old boy sits down in his local and asks the barman,
an old friend, for a drink. The old boy is wearing a
big, old-fashioned stovepipe hat, a black jacket and
waistcoat, and a false, square beard. The barman
serves him a drink and says, "You off to a party
tonight, then?" "Yup," says the man, "I've come as my
love-life." "What are you going on about?" asks the
barman. "You look like Abraham Lincoln." "Indeed
I do," says the man, "my last four scores were seven
years ago!"

∽

Two little old ladies are sitting outside their nursing home having a smoke because it's a no-smoking establishment. It begins to rain and one of them pulls out a condom, cuts the end off and puts it over her cigarette, keeping it nice and dry. The other lady asks her what that thing is. "It's a condom," the little old lady replies. "And where do you get them from?" her friend asks. "Any chemist will sell them to you," the lady replies. The next day, the woman's friend goes off to her local chemist and walks up to the counter. "I'd like some condoms, please, young man," she says to the man behind the counter. "Yes, ma'am," he says, giving her a funny look. "Would you like any particular brand?" "Not really," the little old lady replies, "as long as they'll fit a Camel!"

∞

An old boy walks into an Irish bar in New York with a small dog under his arm. He walks straight up to the bar and puts the dog on it. The barman tells him that animals aren't allowed in the bar and that he'll have to leave. The man says this dog is special, that it can talk and that if anyone wants to bet him $500 he'll take them on. The bartender laughs, but decides to indulge the old guy anyway and takes him up on the bet. So the guy turns to the dog and says slowly,

"Now, Jock, what do we call the thing on top of this bar that keeps the rain off our heads when the weather's bad and the sun off our heads when the weather's good?" The dog shakes his head and then barks, "ROOF!" The barman looks at the man and bursts out laughing. "I'm not paying for that crap – you must be joking!" So the man says, "OK, OK, I'll show you again," and he turns to the dog and says slowly, "Jock, who was the greatest baseball player of all time?" The dog shakes his head and then barks, "RUTH!" The bartender hops over the bar, picks up the dog and the old man, then throws them both out. As they both lie on the sidewalk the dog looks up at the man and says sheepishly, "Should I have said DiMaggio?"

With age comes wisdom. Apparently

A woman went to the surgery. She was seen by one of the new doctors, but after about four minutes in the examination room she burst out, screaming as she ran down the hall. An older doctor stopped and asked what the problem was, and she explained, obviously in shock. The older doctor marched back

to the first and demanded, "What's the matter with
you? Mrs Johnston is 67 years old. She has four
grown children and seven grandchildren, and you told
her she was pregnant?" The new doctor smiled smugly
as he continued to write on his clipboard. "Cured her
hiccups though, didn't I?"

∞

Four people were travelling in the same carriage
on a French train. There was an old, distinguished
lady wearing a fur coat and a haughty expression;
what was probably her granddaughter, a stunning
20-year-old of *Playboy* calibre; a highly decorated
elderly General and a soldier fresh from boot camp.
They spend the time chatting about trivial things,
and then entered a very long tunnel. While in the
tunnel, the sound of a kiss was distinctly heard,
followed by the unmistakable sound of a hand
slapping a cheek. Silence followed, as all were lost in
their respective thoughts. The old lady was thinking:
"Isn't it wonderful that, in this day and age, there are
still young people ready to defend a young woman's
honour?" The young woman was thinking: "How
strange that he'd want to kiss that old hag beside me.
I'm far more attractive!" The General was thinking,
while rubbing his stinging cheek, "It's an outrage that

any woman could think I would try to sneak a kiss in the dark." The soldier had a big grin on his face and was thinking: "Isn't it great that someone can kiss the back of their own hand, then smack an old General in the face and get away with it?"

∞

A young naval student was being grilled by an old sea captain: "What would you do if a sudden storm sprang up on the starboard bow?" "Throw out an anchor, Sir," the student replied. "What would you do if another storm sprang up after?" "Throw out another anchor, Sir." "And if another terrific storm sprang up forward, what would you do then?" asked the Captain. "Throw out another anchor, Sir." "Hold on," said the old Captain, holding up his hand. "Where are you getting all these anchors from?" "From exactly the same place as you're getting your storms, Sir."

Size isn't everything

There's this really vain surfer type. He jogs and he lifts weights, and he stretches and he tones. He's admiring himself in the mirror one day and he notices that all of him looks great apart from his willy – it is the only part of him that doesn't have a tan. So he tries instant tan from all sorts of places and tanning booths, but nothing works. Eventually he goes to see a doctor, who tells him that because of the sensitive nature of the skin, he will only be able to tan his willy in proper sunlight. So the man goes to the beach. Sadly, there are no nudist beaches near where he lives, so he goes to a normal one and tries to get himself a tan without anyone noticing. He can't manage it, so he develops a plan: he digs a hole big enough to hide in and buries himself, apart from his willy, which he leaves sticking out, and leaves a straw up so he can breathe. He puts on suntan lotion and falls asleep. A few minutes later, a couple of little old ladies walk past and one of them notices the willy in the sand. She prods it a couple of times with her walking stick and gets it to wake up a little bit. Then she sighs and says to her friend, "There's no justice, is there?" "What do you mean, dear?" her friend replies. The lady says, "Well, I've spent my life being curious about willies, enjoying them, asking for them, hoping they'll get bigger, and now here I am, 80 years old, and they're growing wild on the beach!"

∞

An old man walks into a bar using a cane and carrying a crocodile. The barman says, "Sorry, mate, no animals allowed in here – especially dangerous ones like that." The man says, "Oh, go on: my croc can do a fantastic trick and it'll have people coming from miles around to see it. Let me show you…" "Well, OK then," says the barman, "but if I think it's crap, I'm going to chuck the pair of you out." So the old man says something to the croc, who gets up on his hind legs and opens his mouth. The man then drops his trousers and puts his pecker into the croc's mouth. The croc shuts its mouth tight around his pecker. The crowd in the bar all gasp out loud, but then the man picks up his cane and raps the croc's head with it three times – tap, tap, tap! The croc opens its mouth and the old man's pecker is there – still attached – without even a scratch on it. Everyone in the bar starts clapping and cheering the old man. "Now," says the old man, looking around the bar, "Does anybody else think they're up to this fantastic trick? Would anyone else like a go?" There is silence and all the men look to the floor. Suddenly an old lady pipes up, "I'll have a try, but you only need to hit me on the head once!"

For years, a little old lady had two monkeys as pets. One day, one of them died of natural causes. Overcome with grief, the second monkey passed away two days later. Not knowing what to do with the remains, she finally decides to take them both to the taxidermist and have them stuffed. After telling the owner of her wishes, he asks her, "Do you want them mounted?" "No, holding hands will be fine," she said, blushing.

∞

An ageing farmer is having trouble with his prize stud bull, which has a herd of 300 cows to sort out. It won't do what is required of it, so the farmer takes it to the vet. Without even examining the animal, the vet hands the farmer a small bottle of pills and says, "Grind one of these into its feed, stand back and watch it go!" Two weeks later, the farmer returns to the vet and says, "Veterinary, that was truly incredible. I did what you said and as soon as he'd eaten the feed, he leaped over the fence and screwed all 300 cows in less than an hour!" The vet says, "So, what's the problem then – why are you back?" The old farmer says, "Well, I was wondering: it's a bit personal, but I've got a hot date with a 30-year-old tonight and I could really do with one of those tablets. I'm not really the man I used to be, after all." "Well, I can't really let you have a whole one," says the vet, "but I guess a quarter of a pill wouldn't do much harm!" So he gives a quarter-pill to the farmer, who goes off to prepare for his date. A few days later, the farmer is back at the vet's again. "What is it this time?" asks the vet. "Well, the pill worked fine – 40 times that one night," says the farmer. "So, what's up, then?" asks the vet. "Well, now I need something for my wrist," says the farmer. "She never turned up!"

An old man had a dog he just loved but that dog had the nasty habit of attacking anything that moved, including people. His friends told him if he had the dog "fixed", he would lose his aggression and quit this behaviour. Thinking it might be a good idea, the old man had his dog fixed. A few days later he was in his front room when the postman came up the steps. The dog jumped up, went right through the door and attacked the postman. The old man ran out, pulled his dog away and began apologizing. "I am so sorry," he said. "I don't know what to do or say. My friends told me he would quit attacking people if I had him fixed, but it didn't work. I just don't know what to do." The postman picked himself up and said, "You should have had his teeth pulled: I knew when he came through the door he wasn't going to hump me."

∞

It was a dark, stormy night. The young soldier was on his first assignment – guard duty. The old General stepped out, taking his dog, a healthy-looking, very strong German Shepherd, for a walk. The nervous young soldier snapped to attention, made a perfect salute and shouted: "Sir, good evening, Sir!" The General, out for some relaxation, returned the salute and said, "Good evening, soldier: nice night, isn't it?" Well, it wasn't a nice night, as it was raining and the soldier had only the standard coat on, while the General had a waterproof overcoat and a pair of gloves, but the Private wasn't going to disagree with the General, so he replied, "Sir, yes, Sir!" The old General continued, "You know, there's something about a stormy night that I find soothing: it's really relaxing. Don't you agree?" The soldier didn't really agree, but then the soldier was just a soldier, and responded, "Sir, yes, Sir!" The General, pointing at the dog, said: "This is a German Shepherd, the best type of dog to train. Very intelligent, very sensitive and very faithful." The private glanced at the dog, saluted yet again and said: "Sir, yes, Sir!" The old General continued, "I got this dog for my wife." The soldier simply said: "Sir, good trade, Sir!"

Money, good looks...

An old soak is looking for a whorehouse and stumbles into a chiropodist's office. He walks up to the front desk and is directed to one of the inspection rooms. Without looking up, the receptionist waves him over to the inspection table and says, "Stick it through the curtain." Thinking, "How cool is this?', the drunken old duffer pulls his plonker out and sticks it through the middle of the curtain. "That's not a foot!" screams the doctor on the other side. "Well, lah-di-dah," says the drunk, "I didn't know there was a minimum!'

❀

There once was a beautiful young woman who wanted to use her good looks to get rich quick. So, she started to hang around older men in the hope of netting one for herself to marry and to shag him to death on their wedding night. Pretty quickly, she found herself a rich 80-year-old, who looked frail, and their romance went quickly and effectively. Three months later it was their wedding day. All went well and in the evening they found themselves in a five-star hotel in Paris. Both retired to their separate bathrooms and she emerged first, seductively dressed, as she slipped between the satin sheets of the huge bed they were about to share. The man's bathroom door opened and he walked out sporting a condom over a 12-inch erection. He was carrying a pair of earplugs and some nose plugs, too. The young woman's heart sank and she began to suspect something was up. Tentatively, she asked, "Er... what are those for, dear?" The old man replied, "These take care of the two things I can't stand the most: the sound of women screaming and the smell of burning rubber!"

∞

A couple have been married for years and years. On their 60th anniversary they decide to go on a second honeymoon. "Let's go to all the same places that we did just after our wedding," the wife says. "Sure," says the husband. "And let's do all the same things that we did just after our wedding," the wife says. "Sure," says the husband. "And we'll make love just like we did after our wedding," the wife says. "Sure," says the husband, "only this time it's me who gets to sit on the side of the bed crying, 'It's too big, it's too big!'"

A funeral service is being held for an ageing woman who has recently died. Right at the end of the service the bearers pick up the coffin and begin to carry it to where it will enter the cremation chamber. As they turn a corner in the chapel the coffin hits the wall and there is a loud, audible "OUCH!" from inside it. They drop the casket to the floor and it turns out that, wonder of all wonders, the woman is actually alive. The old woman lives for two more years and then dies – presumably for real this time. Everyone goes through the same ceremony, but this time, as the bearers round the corner, the woman's husband shouts out, "Careful you lot, watch out for the wall!"

Car trouble

Tiger Woods was having a quiet holiday far away from the sport paparazzi, driving around North Wales in his Volvo. One evening, noticing that he was almost out of petrol, he stopped at a station to fill up. An old man came out from behind an antiquated counter and approached the car. "Fill her up," Tiger Woods said, getting out of the car to stretch his legs. As he did so, a tee fell from his pocket and landed at the feet of the old timer. The attendant picked it up, turned it around in his hands, obviously puzzled, for a full minute. Then, defeated, not able to figure out what it was, he turned to Tiger Woods and asked: "Say, what is this, young man?" "Oh, this is called a tee," the champion golfer answered. Seeing the lack of comprehension in the old timer's eyes, he elaborated: "It's to rest my balls on when I'm taking long drives." The man looked him up and down, then glanced at his car and said admiringly: "They really think of everything at Volvo."

∞

An middle-aged woman had been driving for a marathon 16 hours straight when she decided she'd had enough: she was still at least 6 hours away from her destination, it was almost seven o'clock in the morning and she had dozed off and nearly crashed into a telegraph pole. She decided to pull on to a side road and rest for a bit before carrying on. She turned off the car and closed her eyes... drifting off to sleep, precious sleep... All of a sudden an old man in a bright blue jogging suit knocked on her window, scaring her half to death. "Sorry to wake you," he huffed, jogging in place. "But can you tell me what time it is?" The woman glanced at her watch. "7:15," she said through the glass. "Thank you," the jogger said, and left. "Just my luck," the woman muttered angrily. "I'm parked on someone's jogging route." She considered driving off and parking somewhere else, but she was too tired, so she settled back into the seat, trying to re-capture the beautiful dream she was having... Suddenly another jogger knocked on her window. "Hi, do you have the time?" he said. The woman sighed and looked at her watch. "7:19," she said. "Thanks," the jogger said, then trotted off. She looked down the road and saw more joggers coming her way. Irritated, she retrieved a pen from the glove box and scrawled "I DO NOT KNOW THE TIME" on the back of a magazine. She jammed the hastily-constructed sign in the window with her shoulder and settled back to sleep. Another old jogger knocked on the window just as she started dozing off. The woman pointed at the sign and shouted, "Can't you read?" "Sure I can, madam. I just wanted to let you know that it's 7:27."

A dog's life

A butcher is leaning on the counter towards the close of day when a wee dog with a basket in its jaws comes pushing through the door. "An' wot's this then?" he asks. The dog knocks the basket sharply into the butcher's shins. "You little bugger." As he reaches down to smack the dog, he notices a note and a tenner in the basket. The scribble on the note asks for three pounds of his best mince. The butcher reckons this is too easy. He goes to the window and reaches for the dried-up stuff that's been sitting out all day. The dog growls at him. The butcher turns around and, glaring at the mutt, gets the best mince from the fridge. Weighing out about 2½ pounds, he drops it on the scale with his thumb. "Hmmmmm, a bit shy. Who'll know?" Again, the dog growls menacingly. "Alright, alright," as he throws on a generous half pound. He wraps it up, drops it in the basket and drops in change from a fiver. The dog threatens to chew him off at the ankles. Another fiver goes in the basket. The butcher is quite impressed and decides to follow the little dog home. The dog quickly enters a high-rise building, pushes the lift button, enters the lift, and then pushes the button for the twelfth floor. The dog walks down the corridor and smartly bangs the basket on the door. The door opens, and the dog's elderly owner screams abuse at the dog and then tries to kick it inside. "Hey, what are you doing?" says the butcher. "That's a really smart dog you've got there." "He's a stupid little bugger," says the old guy indignantly. "That's the third time this week he's forgotten his key."

∞

A blind old man with a guidedog at his side walks into a department store. The man walks to the middle of the shop, picks the dog up by the tail and starts swinging it round in circles over his head. The manager, who has seen all this, thinks it a little odd, so he approaches the blind man and says: "Pardon me. May I help you with something?" The blind man says: "No thanks, I'm just looking around."

∞

Given the increase in crime, an old chap goes to a dog-breeder to buy a guard dog, only to be presented with a scruffy terrier mongrel. "What use is that?" he asks. "Ah, but he's a trained killer, this one," promises the breeder. "Watch: Guard dog? That chair!" In a blur of little snappy teeth and yapping, the chair is reduced to splinters. "Amazing!" says the man. "Can I have a go?

Guard dog? That box!" In seconds the box is shredded to mere fluff. Delighted, he buys the mutt and rushes home to show his wife. "Look at our new guard dog," he says. "He's a trained killer!" "What, that thing?" she replies. "Guarddog, my arse!"

Fair trade...

The son of a wealthy older lawyer graduated from college and was considering the future. He went to his father, who had a very large office, and asked if he might be given a desk in the corner where he could observe his father's activities. He could be introduced to his father's clients as a clerk. That way, he could decide whether or not to become a lawyer. His father thought this a splendid idea and this arrangement was set up immediately. On his son's first day at work, the first client in the morning was a rough-hewn man with calloused hands, in workman's attire, who began the conversation by saying: "Mr Lawyer, I work for some people named Gonzales who have a ranch on the east side of town. For many years I have tended their crops and animals, including some cows. I have raised the cows, tended them, fed them, and it has always been my understanding and belief that I was the owner of the cows. Mr Gonzales died and his son has inherited the farm, and he believes that since the cows were raised on his ranch and fed on his hay, the cows are his. In short, we have a dispute as to the ownership of the cows." The lawyer said: "I have heard enough. I will take your case. Don't worry about the cows. The cows will be ours." After the tenant farmer left, the next client came in, a young, well-dressed man, clearly a member of the landed class. "My name is Gonzales. I own a farm on the east side of the town," he said. "For many years, a tenant farmer has worked for my family tending the crops and animals, including some cows. The cows have been raised on my land and fed on my hay, and I believe that they belong to me, but the tenant farmer believes that since he raised them and cared for them, they are his. In short, we have a dispute over ownership of the cows." The lawyer said, "I have heard enough. I will take your case. Don't worry about the cows. The cows will be ours." After the client left, the son came over to his father with a look of concern. "My father, I know nothing of the law, but it seems to me that we have a serious problem regarding these cows." "My darling son, truly, don't worry about the cows," said the old lawyer. "The cows will be ours."

The merchandizing manager of a large food chain was on holiday. While driving through rural Norfolk he developed a headache and decided to stop in the next town and buy some aspirin. Stopping at a small grocery store, he went in and got his aspirin. While in the store, more out of habit than anything else, he walked around to see how it was merchandized. To his amazement, only about two of the ten aisles in the store were devoted to the basic staples and the other eight aisles were filled with salt. He had never seen anything like this in his life and wondered what caused this huge demand for salt in a small rural town in Norfolk. Seeing the proprietor in the rear of the store, he said, "My God, you sell a lot of salt." The old boy shook his head ruefully. "Who, me? Wurr, boy. I don't 'ardly sell no salt at all, but that lad that sells me salt, he sure knows how to sell salt."

There was a country doctor who was the only doctor for miles around. He wanted to go on a fishing trip, so he called the elderly local vet and asked him to look after things while he was gone. The vet asked: "Is anything happening?" The doctor replied, "Mrs Jones is about due, but I don't think the baby will come before I get back. Anyway, if it does, just deliver it. This is her third and the first two went really easily." The old vet said "OK," and the doctor went on the fishing trip. When he returned, he called the vet. "How did things go while I was gone?" "Pretty good." "Did Mrs Jones have her baby?" "Yes, it was an eight-pound boy. Everyone's doing fine." "Did you have any trouble?" "Well, there was just one little problem." "What was that?" "I had a terrible time getting her to eat the afterbirth."

∞

Doctor: "You're in good health. You'll live to be 80."
Patient: "But, doctor, I am 80 right now."
Doctor: "See, what did I tell you?"

∞

Three retired nurses died and went to the Pearly Gates. St Peter asked the first one: "What did you do on Earth that you deserve to get in here? The first nurse replied, "I was an intensive care nurse and I saved hundreds of lives." "Welcome," said St Peter, "come right in. And what did you do?" he asked the second one. The second nurse replied, "I was an emergency room nurse and I saved hundreds of lives." "Welcome," said St Peter, "come right in. And what did you do?" he asked the third one. The third nurse replied, "I was a managed care nurse and I saved the taxpayer hundreds of thousands of pounds." "Welcome," said St Peter, "come right in... but only for three days."

Bits and pieces

An old man is having problems with his dick, which has certainly seen better times. He consults a doctor who, after a couple of tests, says: "Sorry, but you're just not young enough any more. Your dick is burned out. You won't be able to make love more than 12 more times." The man walks home deeply depressed; his wife is already expecting him at the front door and asks him what the doctor said concerning his problem. He tells her what the doctor told him. She says: "Oh my God, only 12 times! We shouldn't waste that; we should make a list." He replies, "Yes, I already made a list on the way home. I'm afraid your name's not on it."

This successful older guy goes to the doctor for a vasectomy. Unlike the usual patients, he shows up in a Rolls-Royce, and sits in the doctor's office in a tuxedo with black tie. The doctor says, "I've done a lot of these, but I've never seen a Rolls and tuxedo before. What's the story?" To which the man responds, "If I'm going to BE impotent, I'm going to LOOK impotent."

∾

A woman starts dating a doctor. Before too long, she becomes pregnant and they don't know what to do. About nine months later, just about the time she is going to give birth, a priest goes into the hospital for a prostate gland infection. The doctor says to the woman: "I know what we'll do. After I've operated on the priest, I'll give the baby to him and tell him it was a miracle." "Do you think it will work?" she asks the doctor. "It's worth a try," he says. So the doctor delivers the baby and then operates on the priest. After the operation he goes in to the priest and says, "Father, you're not going to believe this." "What?" says the priest. "What happened?" "You gave birth to a child." "But that's impossible." "I just did the operation," insists the doctor. "It's a miracle! Here's your baby." About 20 years go by, and the now-elderly priest realizes that he must tell his son the truth while there is still time. One day he sits the boy down and says, "Son, I have something to tell you. I'm not your father." The son says, "What do you mean, you're not my father?" The priest replies, "I'm your mother. The archbishop is your father."

∞

A psychiatrist visited a Norwich mental institution and asked a patient, "How did you get here? What was the nature of your illness?" He got this reply... "Well, it all started when I got married, and I reckon I should never have done it. I married a widow with a grown daughter, who then became my stepdaughter. My dad came to visit us, fell in love with my lovely stepdaughter, then married her. And so my stepdaughter was now my stepmother. Soon, my wife had a son who was, of course, my daddy's brother-in-law, since he is the half-brother of my stepdaughter, who is now, of course, my daddy's wife. So, as I told you, when my stepdaughter married my daddy, she was at once my stepmother. Now, since my new son is brother to my stepmother, he also became my uncle. As you know, my wife is my step-grandmother since she is my stepmother's mother. Don't forget that my stepmother is my stepdaughter. Remember, too, that I am my wife's grandson. But hold on just a few minutes more. You see, since I'm married to my step-grandmother, I am not only the wife's grandson and her hubby, but I am also my own grandfather. Now can you understand how I got put in this place?"

∞

There was an elderly Alabama widow who lived in a large mansion. She was feeling generous when it came to Thanksgiving, so she called up the local military base and asked to speak with the Lieutenant. "Please send up four nice young men to eat dinner here on Thanksgiving, but please, don't send any Jews. Please, no Jews." The Lieutenant replied, "No problem, ma'am, and I am sure I speak for the Army when I say we all appreciate your kindness." Well, Thanksgiving rolled around, and the widow went to answer the door when the bell rang. She was surprised to see four of the blackest boys that anyone had ever seen, especially in the south. "But, but, there must be some mistake," she stammered. One of them replied: "No ma'am. Lieutenant Goldstein doesn't make mistakes."

∞

Three old friends, a Catholic, a Jew and an Episcopalian, all die and reach the Pearly Gates. The Catholic asks to get in and St Peter says, "No, sorry." "Why not?" says the Catholic, "I've been good." "Well, you ate meat on a Friday in Lent, so I can't let you in." The Jew walks up and again St Peter says no. The Jew wants an explanation, so St Peter replies, "There was that time you ate pork... sorry, you have to go to the other place." Then the Episcopalian goes up and asks to be let in, and St Peter again says no. "Why not?" asks the Episcopalian, "What did I do wrong?" "Well," says St Peter, "you once ate your entrée with the salad fork."

∞

The old vicar of a small congregation was trying to find a contractor to paint his church. Because the church fund was low and he couldn't pay very much, he selected the lowest bidder. The contractor decided to make the job pay better by skimping on materials. He thinned the paint with solvent and then only applied one coat. Within months, the poor paint job began to flake away and the church looked worse than it had before the work was done. The old vicar sent a note to the contractor that said: "Repaint, repaint – thin no more!"

Oddbods

A dotty old boy was bothering the waiter in a restaurant. First, he asked that the air conditioning be turned up because he was too hot, then he asked it be turned down because he was too cold, and so on for about half an hour. Surprisingly, the waiter was very patient. He walked back and forth and never once got angry. So finally, a second customer asked him why he didn't throw out the old pest. "Oh, I don't care," said the waiter with a smile. "We don't even have an air conditioner."

∞

Two ageing violinists make a pact that whoever dies first will contact the other and tell him what life in Heaven is like. Poor Max has a heart attack and dies. He manages to make contact with Abe the next day. Abe says: "I can't believe this worked. What's it like in Heaven?" Max replies: "Well, it's great, but I've got good news, and I've got bad news. The good news is that there's a fantastic orchestra up here, and in fact, we're playing 'Scheherazade', your favourite piece, tomorrow night." Abe says: "So what's the bad news?" Max replies: "Well, you're booked to play the solo."

∞

A tourist is sightseeing in a European city. She comes upon the tomb of Beethoven and begins reading the commemorative plaque, only to be distracted by a low scratching noise, as if something were rubbing against a piece of paper. She collars a passing native and asks what the scratching sound is. The local person replies: "Oh, that's Beethoven. He's decomposing."

Age and charm...

There was a Cornish girl who finally found a good job in the city. One night, shortly after arriving in the city, she was invited to a very exclusive party. She didn't know anyone, so she was trying to find someone to talk to when she saw an elegantly-dressed elderly lady standing alone. She approached the lady and said, "Where'm you from?" The lady gave an indignant look and said, "Well! Where I am from, we DON'T end our sentences with a preposition." The young girl immediately replied, "Alright then, where'm you from, bitch?"

Two elderly US army friends decide to have a reunion. One decides to visit the other one, who lives in a big town. The visitor gets lost and calls his friend: "Hey buddy, I *am* coming over, but I'm lost and have no idea where I am." His friend replies: "It's OK, just look at the street intersection, there will be two signs, read them to me." The lost one looks over and then says: "OK, OK, I see them. One says Walk, the other one says Do Not Walk." "Oh good, you're right down the street. I'll come down to fetch you."

∞

A woman in her late fifties arrives home after a shopping trip, and is horrified to find her husband in bed with a pretty, firm young woman. She is about to storm out of the house when her husband stops her by saying, "Honey, before you go, at least give me one chance to explain how on earth this happened!" The woman decides that she owes him this much at least, so stops to listen to his story. He begins, "Well, I was driving home in the pouring rain and I saw this poor thing at the bus stop, soaked. There's a bus strike on, so I offered her a lift and it turned out that she was really hungry. So I brought her home and gave her some of last night's leftovers. I noticed her clothes were shabby so I offered her that jumper you wore once and didn't like and those trousers that don't fit you any more. I noticed her shoes were full of holes, so I gave her a pair of your shoes that you never liked, too. Anyway, just as she was about to leave she asked me, 'And is there anything else that your wife doesn't use any more?' So here we are!"

An old guy walks into a bar and orders a double whisky – straight. As he begins to drink he reaches into his wallet and pulls out a photograph. He takes a quick peek at it and then puts it back quickly in his wallet. He then finishes his whisky, calls the barman over and orders another. He begins to drink it, and as he does so, he reaches into his wallet and pulls out the photograph again, looks at it and then puts it quickly away. He continues doing this for about an hour. Eventually the barman asks him, "Hey mate, what's with the photo? I'm not worried by the amount you're drinking, I'd just really like to have a look at the picture – what on earth is it?" The old man replies, "It's a photograph of my wife. When she starts to look good, I know it's time to go home!"

It's a beautiful day in County Kerry and people all over the county are sitting outside the pubs enjoying stout by the pint. In a cosy pub, one old chap turns to his friend and says, "You see that old boy over there?" His friend nods. "Have you noticed that he's the spitting image of me? It's bloody uncanny, that's what it is, to be sure. I'm going to go over there and ask him a few questions: after all, 'tis not every day that you get to meet someone who could be your exact double, now is it?" And off he goes to see the man he is talking about. He taps him on the shoulder and says, "Excuse me, I couldn't help noticing from over there that you look almost exactly the same as me. I was thinking what an incredible coincidence that was!" "Me too, me too," replies the man, "I noticed you earlier and I was just about to come over and talk when I saw you coming over anyway. 'Tis an incredible thing, to be sure. So whereabouts are you from?" he asks. "Well, I'm from Galway, originally," says the first old man. "No, that's incredible!" says the second, "Me too! It's just unbelievable. What street did you live in?" "Why, I lived in Moher Street for 20 years, so I did," comes the reply from the first man. "No! I can't believe it – I did, too," says the second. "And what number in that street was it?" he asks. "Why, I lived in number 20." "Unbelievable," comes the reply, "that's the number I lived in. And what were your parents' names?" "Ruari and Siobhan," comes the reply. "This really is uncanny," the first man says, "those are the exact names of my parents, too!" At this point, the bar staff turn up for the next shift. The new guy asks, "Anything happening?" and the guy who is about to go replies, "No, not really; just the Rix twins being drunk again!"

Doctor, doctor

An old man goes to the doctor with a strange problem. "Doctor, whenever I break wind there is no smell at all. It's really strange, and no matter what I eat, I get the same result – no smell whatsoever!" The doctor has a cursory investigation and then asks the man if he can possibly break wind there and then. The old man drops his trousers and pants, and farts extremely loudly. The doctor sniffs at the air a couple of times and immediately says, "Oh yes, this is a common one. I know exactly what the problem is," and he walks out of the room. He comes straight back with a six-foot pole with a large brass hook on the end. "Doctor! What the heck are you going to do with that pole?" asks the old man. "I'm going to open the window," says the doctor. "You've got a blocked nose!"

∞

An ageing man goes to a doctor and, twitching his fingers and stuttering, finally manages to say, "Doctor, I have a... er... sexual performance problem. Can you help me?" "Oh, that's not a problem for us men any more!" announces the proud physician with a broad wink. "This new pill just came out – a new wonder drug called Miagra. That does the trick! You take a few of these and it's the end of your problems!" So the doctor gives the man a prescription for a packet of Miagra and sends him on his merry way. A couple of months later, the doctor runs into his patient on the street. He's pleased to notice that the man is looking slimmer, better-groomed and all-round happier. "Doctor, doctor!" exclaims the man excitedly, "I've got to thank you! This drug is a miracle! It's wonderful!" "Well, I'm glad to hear that," says the physician, rather pleased with himself. "And what does your wife think about it?" "*Wife?*" says the guy with a silly grin on his face. "I haven't been home yet!"

∞

A rather embarrassed 50-something man goes to see his doctor and tells him: "Well, I have this problem. You see, I can't get it up for my wife anymore, if you know what I mean." "It's quite all right," the doctor says. "Get undressed and we'll see what the problem is." He does so, but can find nothing wrong with the patient. "Come back tomorrow," he advises. "Bring your wife with you. I'd like to examine her, too." The anxious patient turns up the following day with his wife, as promised. The doctor has a quick look at the woman, then asks her to take her clothes off. "Mmm... I see... Now turn around, please. Mmmm... Can you crouch down for me? That's it. Gooooood, now get on all fours on the carpet. Yes, this way... Mmmm... It's OK, you can put your clothes back on." While the wife is getting dressed, the doctor takes the husband aside and tells him: "You're perfectly healthy. Don't worry. Your wife didn't give me an erection either."

Old dogs...

The old General arrived at his office on a Sunday morning and discovered that none of his private aides was there. Grimly, he remembered it had been one aide's birthday party the previous evening and

he had no doubt as to what condition they were in.
At around ten o'clock, five aides arrived, unshaven
and dressed in rather piteous attire. They saluted as
smartly as they could and braced themselves for the
old General's grilling. "I presume you were at Smith's
birthday party last night, weren't you?" "Sir, yes, Sir,"
one aide answered. "And you couldn't get up early
enough this morning to get to the office because you
were too drunk!" thundered the General. "Er, no,
Sir," the aide said timidly, looking at his friends. "So
what is your excuse, young man?" the old General
wondered, sitting down, with a dangerous, vicious
smile on his lips. "I can explain. You see, we did run
a little late, I admit. We ran to the bus but we missed
it; we hailed a cab but it broke down; we found a
farm and bought eight horses but they dropped dead;
we ran ten miles, and now we're here. It's just a
logistical problem, really, General, Sir!" The General
eyed him suspiciously, but as he hadn't heard such a
good one for a long time, he let the men go. An hour
later, the last aide showed up, in the same dishevelled
state. "Sorry, Sir," he said. "I ran late; tried to catch
a bus but missed it; I hailed a cab but..." "Let me
guess," the old General interrupted. "The cab broke
down, so you bought a horse in a farm but it died on
you, so you ran for ten miles. Do you really think I'm
going to swallow this?" "Er, no, Sir. You see, there

were so many dead horses on the way that it took forever to go round them."

❧

Four retired friends decide to go golfing. One of them pays the fees, while the other three go up to tee off. They are all bragging about their sons. The first man says, "Well, my son's in construction, and he's so successful that he gave one of his friends a brand-new house for free." The second man says, "Well, my son's a car salesman, and he's so successful that he gave one of his friends a Porsche for free." The third man says, "Well, my son's a stockbroker, and he's so successful that he gave one of his friends a share portfolio for free." At this point the fourth man arrives on the scene and they tell him, "We were just discussing how our sons are doing. Is yours successful?" The man says, "Well, my son is gay, and he's an erotic dancer in a gay bar." There is a silence as the others look embarrassed for the man. "I'm not really thrilled about the dancing, but still," the man continues, "he does pretty well anyway. His boyfriends recently had a bit of a competition among themselves and gave him a share portfolio, a Porsche and a brand-new house, all for free!"

❧

Nikos, a wizened old Greek man, was sitting in a bar talking to a young tourist. "So," he says, "you see that wall out there in that field?" He points to a huge stone wall separating two fields. "Can you see how well it's built? I spent three years of my life moving stones from down in the valley up to those pastures and carving them so they fitted. That's the strongest fence between here and Athens! And do they call me Nikos the wall-builder? No, they do not!" Then he continues, "So, you see the bar here? The one you are leaning on, right now?" and he raps it with his knuckles. 'Can you see how well it's built? I spent a year of my life cutting, sanding and waxing this bar. This is the finest bar between here and Athens! And do they call me Nikos the bar-builder? No, they do not!" Then he continues, "So, you see the pier out there in the water?" He points to a long, solid pier that stretches out into the deep, deep water. "I spent five long years of my life putting that pier together. I cut down the trees, I nailed the boards and I dug the holes for the poles. It almost killed me, and it is the finest pier between here and Athens! And do they call me Nikos the pier-builder? No, they do not!" Then he looks around and checks the bar before he continues, "So, I screw one lousy goat...!"

A man is confused about sex and the Sabbath day. He just cannot work out whether having sex on the Sabbath is a sin or not, because he doesn't know whether it is work or play. He goes to see his local priest and asks him for his opinion on this question. The priest gets his Bible down and flicks through it, reading a passage here and a passage there. Eventually he tells the man, "Well my son, after consulting the Good Book, I have decided that sex is probably closer to work, and therefore you should not practise it on the Sabbath." The man thanks the priest, but as that wasn't really the answer he was looking for, he decides to go and see the local minister, who is married and may see things a bit more his way. He asks the minister the question and, to his disappointment, the minister gives him the same answer as the priest, "No sex on the Sabbath." The man decides to go and see another type of holy man – the wise old local Rabbi. The Rabbi is asked the question and he ponders it over. Eventually he says, "Well my son, I have come to the conclusion that sex is definitely play so therefore you can have sex on the Sabbath." The man says, "That's great, Rabbi, but how do you come to that conclusion when so many others disagree?" The Rabbi thinks a little and then says quietly, "If sex were work, my wife would get the maid to do it!"

Jake moves to Australia after working all his life in the City. He buys a farm in the remotest part of the Outback he can find. His post arrives once a week, his groceries once a month and he can call the Flying Doctor on his radio if he has an emergency. One night, after six months of this, Jake is finishing his dinner when he hears a knock on the door. He walks up, opens it and sees a huge, grizzled old outbacker standing in front of him. "G'day, mate," says the outbacker. "I'm your nearest neighbour, Bruce Sheldon, from 20 miles east. I'm having a party Saturday night and I thought you might like to come along, mate." "That'd be great," says Jake. "I haven't really spoken to anyone for six months. Thanks a lot." Bruce is about to turn away, but instead says, "I think I'd better warn you, though: there'll be some serious drinking going on." "Not a problem," says Jake, "I like a couple of pints myself." Bruce is about to turn away again, but instead says, "Better warn you, though, there'll probably be some fighting, too." "Not a problem," says Jake, "I know how to keep out of trouble." Bruce is about to turn away again, but instead says, "Better warn you, though, there'll probably be some pretty wild sex, too." "Not a problem," says Jake, "I've been alone for six months, remember? Now, what time should I show up?" Bruce turns once more and says, "Whenever you like, mate. There's only going to be me and you there anyway!'

∞

An old man has been on a desert island for twenty years. One day, while he is knee-deep in the sea spearing a fish, he notices a strange movement in the water. A few minutes later, a few feet away from him, a gorgeous woman in a tight wet suit stands up. Dumbfounded, he simply watches her approach, dripping with water, teeth flashing, hips swaying. "How long has it been since you last had a cigarette?" she asks in a throaty voice. "My dear, it's been decades," the old chap answers in a shaky voice. The woman diver opens the zip of her breast pocket and fishes out a packet of cigaretes and a lighter. She places a cigarette in his mouth and lights it. She lets the man take a drag and then asks: "How long has it been since you last had a nice Scotch?" "A long, long time," the old man replies, holding his breath. The woman pulls down the front zip of her wet suit, just enough to reach down and bring out a bottle of whiskey. She places her hands around the neck and gently twists the cap open. She takes a swig, licks the liquid on her lips and passes the bottle to the guy and then asks, her finger toying suggestively with her front zip, "Tell me, how long has it been since you last played around?" "My God," breathes the old boy. "Don't tell me you have golf clubs in there, too!"

Classic Quotes

I asked my wife, "Where do you want to go for our anniversary?" She said, "Somewhere I've never been!" I told her, "How about the kitchen?"

Henny Youngman

I'm looking forward to being properly old: really old, so that I can lean over in a restaurant and say to my son, "You know what I just did? I just pissed myself.... You deal with it!"

Dylan Moran

In my lifetime I saw the Berlin Wall come and I saw it go. George Burns can say the same thing about the Ice Age.

Bob Hope

Dorothy: Age is just a state of mind.
Blanche: Tell that to my thighs.

The Golden Girls

Nice to be here? At my age it's nice to be anywhere.

George Burns

Happiness is having a large, loving, caring, close-knit family – in another city.

George Burns

A sexagenarian? At his age? That's disgusting.

Gracie Allen

I don't need you to remind me of my age. I have a bladder to do that for me.

Stephen Fry

In the Czech Republic, some drunken friends accidentally drank their grandfather's ashes mistaking them for instant coffee. They realised their mistake when they noticed that the coffee tasted of Werther's Originals.

Have I Got News for You

I said to my wife, "If I ever get like that – y'know, mumbling to myself and shitting my pants – shoot me!" She said, "Better start running, monkey boy!"

Lee Evans

When I was a boy the Dead Sea was only sick.

George Burns

It feels great to be nearly 100: I mean, for those parts of me that still have feeling.

Bob Hope

He's so old that when he orders a three-minute egg, they ask for the money up front.

Milton Berle

I'm so old they've cancelled my blood type.

Bob Hope

I knew I was going bald when it was taking longer and longer to wash my face.

Harry Hill

Everything that goes up must come down, but there comes a time when not everything that's down can come up.

George Burns

I think women spend far too much money going into Boots and buying all this anti-wrinkle cream to slap on their faces to make them look younger, and it doesn't work. You might just as well slap a bit of fruit cake mix on your face, go out in the sun for two hours, then at least you've got a cake to show for it.

Jo Brand

It is said that at the age of 55 each man becomes what he most despised at the age of 25. I live in constant fear lest I become a badly organised trip to Bournemouth.

Simon Munnery

Talk about getting old, I was getting dressed and a peeping tom looked in the window, took a look and pulled down the shade.

Joan Rivers

If a woman tells you she's 20 and looks 16, she's twelve. If she tells you she's 26 and looks 26, she's damn near 40.

Chris Rock

Saffy: Mountaineers have died falling into shallower ravines than your wrinkles!

Absolutely Fabulous

Middle age is when your age starts to show around your middle.

Bob Hope